TRUE & REASONABLE

Doug Jacoby

PUBLICATIONS INTERNATIONAL

One Merrill Street
Woburn, MA 01801
1-800-727-8273
Fax (617) 937-3889

True and Reasonable

First Edition copyright © 1988
Central London Church of Christ
London, England.

Second Edition copyright © 1992
Greater Philadelphia Church of Christ
Philadelphia, Pennsylvania, USA.

Third Edition copyright © 1994
Discipleship Publications International.

ISBN 1-884553-22-2

To Vicki, my wife
and best friend.

Table of Contents

5

Preface

Why I Wrote The Book

Many books have been written to defend the Christian faith. The area of religion concerned with showing that the Christian faith is reasonable is called "evidences" or "apologetics."

I have noticed that most evidences books assume the reader has a good general knowledge of Christianity. While this may be the case for many readers, more and more people with little Christian background are investigating Christianity. Many have never opened a Bible, attended a church service, or had a friend who was personally committed to Christ.

Furthermore, the plurality of the foremost apologetic works promulgate a veritable cornucopia of sophisticated vocabulary, thereby obfuscating the intended message(!).

This book makes few assumptions—either about the reader's religious background or language skills. After all, the Bible is written for everyone to understand—from the man in the street to the university professor. This book is not meant to be "deep" or academic. It is my conviction that we do not have to be deep or particularly clever to get the message across (John 7:15, Acts 4:13, 1 Corinthians 2:1-5, 2 Corinthians 1:13).

So if you want depth, turn to the Suggested Reading at the end of the book, and in the meantime enjoy the book as a refresher.

The truth is that the Christian faith is reasonable, as this book will attempt to demonstrate. It is logical, it makes sense, and it works! No one who has seriously examined it can walk away and say "Nonsense!"

Becoming a Christian is not primarily a matter of upbringing, experiences, or individual preference. It is a personal response to evidence. With this in mind, we must examine the evidence—many are unaware how strong it is!—and then make a decision. You see, believing the evidence is not enough; a response is what God is looking for.

This book has been written to bring us to a saving faith in Jesus Christ. In order for that to occur, three things must happen:

- We must be convinced of the reality of God.
- We must be convinced of the truth of the Bible.
- We must make an informed decision about Jesus.

If you are like I once was, you may have believed that there is a God—or hoped so—but being unaware of the evidence, you have had doubts. Since true faith is in the heart and not just in the head, we must be convinced of the reality of God:

> And without faith it is impossible to please God, because anyone who comes to him must believe that he exists and that he rewards those who earnestly seek him (Hebrews 11:6).

Believing that God exists is essential, and so Section I of the book shows that the existence of God is reasonable.

To be convinced that the Bible is God's word, or message to us, we need more than a casual acquaintance with it. We need to explore, to open our hearts and minds, and then we will see that God's message to man is both true and reasonable. With this in mind, Section II of the book covers a number of issues related to the trustworthiness of the Bible.

In the concluding chapter, we are urged to make an informed decision. It is my prayer that by the time you reach the end of the book, your personal conviction will be that Christianity is both **True and Reasonable.**

SECTION I

GOD

In the first five chapters of the book we examine fundamental questions about God that people have asked for centuries—and which have been well answered. The first two chapters deal with the existence of God, while the third explores his personality. The fourth and fifth chapters explain what God has done for us in his Son, Jesus Christ, and how he speaks to us in his message to mankind, the Bible. These elementary matters are the logical starting point for a book on the reasonableness of the Christian faith.

CHAPTER ONE

Clearing Away the Debris

Arguments Against the Reality of God

I can't see "God" anywhere in the heavens!
—Yuri Gagarin, Soviet Cosmonaut, 12 April 1961.

THE UNREALITY OF GOD

FEW ATHEISTS ARRIVED AT THEIR BELIEFS BY SERIOUSLY EXAMINING the evidence for God's existence. Most atheists became atheists because they could not relate to "God"—at least not to "God" as some people portrayed him. Maybe they had bad experiences with organized religion. Or maybe they saw no valid reasons for faith, and sensed the immense hypocrisy in those who claim to know God. For many it was personally inconvenient to accept the reality of God and his authority in their lives, so they concluded there was probably no God after all! Later, after concluding there was no God, they then thought of some reasons why, working backwards from their conclusion that he could not exist.

In this chapter we will look at some of the (illogical) reasons people have concluded that there is no God. Because there's so much confusion about the issue of God's existence, we need to clear away the debris before building up a convincing case for the existence (or reality) of God.

LACK OF "PROOF"

When the Soviet cosmonaut spoke the words quoted above, he had become the first Russian—and the first human being—to go into outer space. His concept of God was wrong, so when he looked for visible proof of God's existence, he didn't find any. Perhaps he would have been pleased to see a large metallic throne orbiting the earth directly over Jerusalem!

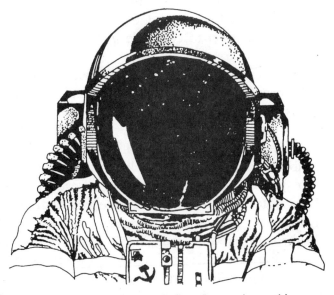

Ya neegdye nye veeju "bogu" na nyebyesach!

When most people say there's no "proof" for the existence of God, they are making the same mistake the Russian cosmonaut made. They are looking for scientific proof—like footprints or a photograph. But they misunderstand the nature of God, as we will see in Chapter 3. He isn't a man, so there will be no footprints. He isn't even a physical being, so don't expect any photographs!

A number of real physical things can't be seen with the eye—for example, electricity, sound waves and protons. Even though we cannot see them, they still exist, and we understand their properties. No one would deny that electricity is real, especially after an electric shock! It's the same with God. He is real, and his presence can be detected through studying his influence on the world. He is invisible, but real all the same.

Yes, many things are real—they exist—even though they can't be measured scientifically. Half of reality is physical, but the other half is spiritual. It would be as inappropriate to try to photograph God as to mark out two miles of justice, or to weigh three pounds of love. Love doesn't come in pounds, but it is absolutely incorrect to conclude that therefore love is unreal.

Is there no proof of God? Of course there is! There is a great deal of proof, but not direct scientific proof as such. Yet the proof is just as convincing, if we are open to being convinced. A court of law does not throw out the testimony of a witness just because he is lacking photographic evidence.

The Bible is not an evidences book. No, the Bible does not attempt to "prove" God—it assumes we already know he exists. The greatest evidence for God is the lives of those who are really following him. God is known through his action in the world, through his Son, through his Word, and through his life-changing Spirit in the hearts of men and women around the world. The nature of God is the subject of our next chapter, and we will resume the discussion there.

HYPOCRISY

"Since most people who believe in God are hypocrites— they don't practice what they preach—what they believe in must not be true." At least this is how many people think. The error of this way of thinking should be clear to all. A doctor may be a smoker, and obviously this is unwise medically, but that doesn't mean he is incompetent as a physician. A salesman may be greedy and even dishonest, but that doesn't mean that his company's product is worthless—he is just a poor representative. In the same way, many who claim to be Christians today are poor representatives of a good religion!

Often people ask about the Crusades, when "Christians" forcibly baptized throngs of "infidels" or unbelievers. Or about the Inquisition, when the Roman Catholic Church relied on torture to bring about uniformity in religious opinion. Those responsible were certainly terrible representatives of their religion, but the abuses of Christianity do not prove that this was Christ's intention . The Crusaders who killed in the name of Jesus and the Inquisitors who tortured in the name of truth were seriously mistaken, but they are not an embarrassment to true Christians—only an example of obvious abuses. It is good to spread the faith (in fact it's commanded), but not at sword point! It is good to persuade people to have correct views—but not through fire and the rack!

Hypocrisy among "Christians" does not show the falsehood of Christ's teachings—only the great need for them to be properly put into practice! Certainly we see that the sad fact of hypocrisy has nothing at all to do with the existence of God!

SUFFERING

Perhaps the most serious objection to God's existence is the presence of suffering in the world. Since there is so much suffering in the world, either God is good but not all-powerful (since he cannot prevent evil), or all-powerful but not good (since he doesn't prevent suffering). This argument against the existence of God—or the existence of a good, all-powerful God—is a weak one. Since so much suffering is inflicted by humans (war, drunk driving, stealing, lying...), to root out all suffering God would have to destroy all evil in the world.

But consider for a minute what would happen if God did eliminate all suffering in the world: to completely root out evil he would have to destroy us! As for evil actions, our decisions would be overruled, and we would become preprogrammed puppets. And how about evil thoughts?—our brains would be wiped clean. Now would it really be better to live in a world without choice, without free will? Would it really be better to live as creatures without personality? Or to feel no pain? (Pain has its benefits: teaching caution, keeping us away from danger, building character, et cetera.)

What if the Bible is true? What if eternity awaits Christians after death? Imagine you lived seventy years in absolute agony, fighting arthritis, migraines, ulcers, cancer, et cetera. Terrible suffering! Then you die, the suffering is ended, and you spend eternity (forever) in heaven with God. How much of your suffering on earth do you think you would remember after 7,000 years in heaven? After 7,000,000 years? How strong do you think the memory would be after 7,000,000,000,000,000 years? The fact is, the only thing that counts is going to heaven; no length of suffering on earth will seem significant compared to the time we will spend with God afterwards.

Even if you do not believe in God or "eternity," you will recognize that the problem of suffering wouldn't be too big a problem for God, and certainly it isn't a good argument against his existence. And remember, if you really wanted God to weed evil out of the world—before the Day of Judgment—we would all be destroyed along with it!

But perhaps you are thinking there is another option: God could have decided not to create the world in the first place. Why did he take a chance on a being so risky as man, and on a world that would become so devastated by man's selfishness (wars, pollution, divorce...)? If this is your question, then let it be asked why we decide to have children. Can we be absolutely sure that our children will turn out perfectly? Or that they will not disappoint us, or even worse, become criminals? Then why do we take the risk?

For love. The Christian scriptures teach that God created man so that he could love us. God desires children to love. Because he is lonely? No, but because he is good, and wants to share his love. Whether we enjoy that love or abuse the free will he has given us is our decision, but let's not blame God for our mistakes.

ABSURD QUESTIONS

Some people think they can dismiss the vital question of God's existence by asking tricky questions: Let's consider two questions often asked:

- If God created everything, who created God?
- Could God create a rock so big that he couldn't move it?

As for the first question, the reasoning is that either (a) God created himself, which is ridiculous (how can nothing create something?), or (b) some other being created God, in which case God is not really "God," for if he were really God he wouldn't need someone to create him. The question is misleading, because it assumes that everything must have a creator. The first question could be rewritten:

> If God created everything, and everything has a creator, then who created God?

Of course the idea that God exists is ridiculous if he had to create himself, or if he isn't really "God" because a being superior to him must have created him. (In that case another question must be asked: Who created the being that created God?) But why is it necessary that everything have a creator? Why should the creator be part of the creation ? Is the artist a part of his painting? Or the architect a part of the building he designed? Then why should God, who by definition is the (original) creator, be part of the universe? You see, people who ask the question have made a huge assumption. It's somewhat like the question:

> Have you stopped beating your wife yet?

Unless you are guilty, a yes/no answer will not do. The question assumes that you are guilty. In the same way, many questions about God assume things about him that are completely false. In fact, God is outside of time (Luke 20:38), so attempts to limit him to our world of space and time will always introduce a false concept of God. Maybe the husband never was beating his wife, and maybe God was not created— or always was.

Now, about God's ability to create a rock too large for him to move, this is a similar sort of question, though the solution is more difficult. Apparently God does limit himself: if he did everything within his power, he could create and destroy each of us constantly, move galaxies and planets about at random, et cetera. But what would be the point? (God is a God of order.) But the question of God's ability to limit himself is not the real question here. Let's take another look at the original question:

> Could God create a rock so big that he couldn't move it?

The question is inappropriate. It is against reason to ask it, since it would be absolutely impossible for God to create a rock so big that he couldn't move it. Does that mean that God isn't God? No, but you must understand what I mean by "absolutely" impossible.

Some things are absolutely impossible, others are only relatively impossible. It is relatively impossible for a man to lift a car over his head—no man is strong enough. (At least I don't know anyone who could do this, though this could be imagined). But what about the immovable rock? That is impossible logically. That is, even for an all-powerful being,

it couldn't be done, because it would require a violation of logic and truth. God cannot be untrue to himself.

Here are some other things that are absolutely impossible: loud silence, boiling ice, a nineteen-ounce pint. You see, all these things are impossible by definition, or absolutely impossible—but that says nothing about the existence of God.

Complicated, you may be thinking. Why don't we agree that the question was absurd? If you want a good short answer to the rock question, here it is:

> Maybe, but he could certainly build a bulldozer big enough to do the job.

In short, there's never been a logical question that has disproven the existence of God. Moreover, most such questions fail to take into account God's true nature. By logic alone it is as impossible to disprove God's existence as to prove it. Logic is only a tool.

"RELIGIOUS" TRUTH

When we were children we learned to distinguish truth from falsehood, and, in time, reality from imagination. Certain things were true, while others were false, or make-believe. In our minds, we put the true ideas into the "true" box, the false ones into the "false" box. For example, many of us were taught to believe in Santa Claus or Father Christmas, Kwan Yin or Krishna, the Tooth Fairy or the Easter Bunny—imaginary beings in whom it was nice to believe. (Many of us were also taught to believe in God.) All these beings were "true," or "real" to us at the time, and so we put them into the "true" box.

As we grew older and wiser, we became "unbelievers" in these make-believe beings, and our beliefs matured. We didn't blame friends or parents for leading us "astray"—after all, there was no harm in make-believe, and it had been nice to believe in these beings. We simply took these concepts or ideas out of the "true" box and put them into the "false" box. Eventually, our ideas about God and his reality were challenged as well— we found that lots of "nice" people, including famous people and scientists, don't believe in God, and we could not answer their questions. So just as with imaginary animals, ghosts, the Bogey Man and Santa Claus, it was time for re-evaluation.

But would it be right to put "religious" truths into the "false" box? That would be awkward, since so many adults live

19

their lives by their religious convictions (not the case with Santa Claus!), and this might offend them. One thing, however, was certain: "God" must not remain in the "true" box. So what could we do?

We created a third box, one for "religious" truth. It wasn't exactly true (maybe "true" for you, but not necessarily "true" for me), and yet it wasn't false, either (since so many people strongly believed in it). Thus "religious" truth, somewhere between "true" truth and falsehood, became the realm of God, the supreme being in the fairyland of "religion".

There is one problem with all of this. Exactly what is religious truth: true or false? Is there really a God, or not? It's fine to "believe" in God if you don't seriously care to answer the question, but what if you do want real answers? For modern man, "religious truth" is confused with religious ideas. Since intolerance is unpopular, we are willing to grant that all religious ideas are "true"—provided, of course, that they are not too extreme.

This is not to say that people aren't entitled to their religious beliefs, only that it's nonsense to say all ideas are equally valid. (How can all ideas be equally valid when they contradict each other?) This confused way of looking at truth, popular with many and promoted by clergymen, priests and theologians, must be wholly abandoned if we are to reach a sensible conclusion about God's existence. Is he real, or not?

Modern man is confused about faith. He thinks that faith creates truth. That is, if you believe it, it is true (at least for you). If you believe in heaven and hell, fine. It may be real for you, but not for me—I don't look at things that way. Whether heaven and hell exist may be debated, but ultimately either they exist or they don't. I have met men so deluded that they claimed to be Jesus Christ himself. Is that possible? Of course not. But what if they were truly sincere? Then they would be sincerely wrong—but wrong nevertheless.

No, faith does not create truth. Faith can be completely mistaken about what is true, and we can place our faith in the wrong thing. For example, it would certainly be better to have a weak faith in a strong bridge than a strong faith in a weak bridge. Christians could be wrong about the strength of their bridge, but they do not pretend that the bridge exists only for those who believe it is there.

Whether or not you believe in him has no bearing on God's existence. If he exists, he exists, and no amount of believing can change the fact. In the same way, if he is not really there, no amount of faith can change that fact. Strong belief does not give us the power to flap our arms and fly, nor does it allow us to conjure up a God who exists only in our "heart" or imagination.

Yes, the question of truth is a crucial one. Indeed, many of us are unbelievers today because society avoids the question of truth by speaking of "religious truth" instead. Religious ideas must be able to stand the test of criticism—after all, they are either true or false. If they are so delicate that serious investigation would topple them, they probably aren't true anyway.

This is also the position of the Bible. As the apostle Paul insisted to Governor Festus, the truth about Christ is "true and reasonable" (Acts 26:25). Few religions invite you to examine their claims as Christianity does.

PERSONAL DISTANCE

Probably the major reason why we find it hard to believe in God, or that God seems unreal to us, is our own lifestyle. We fill our lives with so many other things that we have no time for God, and so he seems distant. (No wonder! My wife would seem a bit distant too if I only talked to her once a week, or when I was in trouble, felt lonely, or needed a good meal!) Moreover, for millions of people, believing in God wouldn't be very convenient, so they deny the existence of God and justify

21

it with some philosophical technicality, or complaint about his justice, or some "contradiction" supposed to exist in the Bible.

The real issue is that we do not want to change. Yet God won't force us to follow him; it's our decision. Does God exist? Absolutely. Does he seem distant, or unreal? Perhaps it's because we prefer it that way.

CONCLUSION

No atheist has ever produced a solid argument against the existence of God. In nearly every case where someone has decided there is no God, the underlying reason for that decision is the inconvenience that would result to that person's life if he decided that God really exists. Not to say that God's existence depends on our decision. He is there whether or not we choose to live for him.

Now that we have cleared away some of the debris—notions that cloud our understanding—we're in a better position to consider the evidence for the existence of God.

Chapter Two

Is Anyone At Home?

Evidences For the Reality of God

I n the previous pages we have examined a number of reasons people don't believe there is a God: lack of "proof," religious hypocrisy, suffering in the world, absurd questions, confused notions of truth, and the personal inconvenience of surrendering our lives to God. We needed to discuss these matters before moving on. But now that we have cleared away the debris—invalid reasons against the existence of God—we are in a position to examine some of the positive proof that there must be a God.

All that we established in the first chapter is that there could be a God—that there are no particularly good arguments against his existence. But if there is anyone at home in the universe, there should be some pointers to his existence. And so there are! This chapter will explore a number of areas which point to the fact of God's existence.

THE ARGUMENT FROM DESIGN

If there is a design, there must be a designer. If there is natural law in the world, there must be a law-giver. If there is structure and consistency in the creation, there must be a Creator. That is the argument in its simplest form.

The most common illustration is that of the watch. Suppose you are walking through the woods and notice in the leaves a watch. You would certainly assume that someone had lost it, and that the watch originally was made by a watchmaker. Since the universe is incredibly more complicated than the watch, we must assume that it has a maker.

If I suggested that there was no watchmaker, but that a colony of squirrels had made it, you would laugh, saying that it was too complicated to be made by a being so simple and unintelligent as a squirrel. If I claimed that it just "happened," over a very long period of time and through natural processes, you would think I was joking, and besides, it's much too complex to be the product of random forces. If I said that it was created by no one, but had always existed, you would correctly reply that if that were the case it would have stopped ticking ages ago.

Now which is more complicated: the watch or the whole universe? Obviously the clockwork universe is much too complex to have been created by a being of lower intelligence like man. Much too complicated to have come into existence by itself. Much too orderly and well-running to have always existed.

The most reasonable explanation is that **God created the universe.** What does this have to do with the existence of God? If there is a universe, there must be a God. It's that simple.

A word of caution: some people speak of evolution as though it accounts for everything we see in the world today: "Evolution is true, so who needs God?"—so the argument goes. In fact, the theory of evolution has never been proven. True, scientists have shown that evolutionary change has occurred within existing life forms to some extent at certain levels throughout history. But this in no way means that evolution is the means by which life came into existence.

THE FACT OF EVOLUTION

Life forms have developed and diversified into new life forms. This sort of limited evolution continues to occur today.

THE THEORY OF EVOLUTION

Life arose from non-life, and all life forms today can be accounted for by evolutionary change from simpler to more complex organisms. Life began in a single cell and "evolved" to the present situation.

In short, the **fact** of evolution must not be confused with the **theory** of evolution. The "theory of evolution" is that evolution as we understand it accounts for all life forms today. (In other words, my great, great, great, great, great, great, great,...great-grandfather was a simple single-celled organism in the primitive ocean.) But evolutionary change here and there must not be taken to prove that evolution brought the world into existence, changed raw chemicals into simple life forms, and then transmuted these simple creatures into more complex ones, including man. Although there is ample proof that evolution occurs on a limited scale today, there is no proof that evolutionary principles account for all life today. The theory of evolution is theory, not fact!

Study the evidence for yourself. You may be surprised to learn that, at best, the theory of evolution is a guess at how we came to be. It has not been proven, it cannot be proven, and besides, it is riddled with difficulties. Virtually any scientist, when pressed, will admit that the theory of evolution is an unproved theory.

You may be wondering, "If the theory of evolution isn't true, why is it that most educated people believe it?" Why? Probably for the same reason that most uneducated people believe it: since it is usually presented as the only explanation of the origin of life, few have taken the time to look into other explanations. Understand that the theory of evolution has no bearing whatsoever on the existence of the universe; it only attempts to explain what has happened from the beginning until now.

The evolutionist actually needs more "faith" to believe his theory (that is, he must make more assumptions, many of which are highly questionable) than the person who believes in a creator. The evolutionist thinks, by stretching out the assumptions over millions and millions of years, that this somehow makes them more plausible. The argument from design is a more sound and likely explanation than the theory of evolution. There is a God, and he is the creator. The universe, for those who are willing to see God's hand in it, is an overwhelming pointer to the existence of God!

SPIRITUAL EXPERIENCE

Where did the idea or concept of God come from? Why is it found all over the world? Why is it that the most primitive peoples believed in one God (not many), while as "civiliza-tion" developed men created more and more gods? The influence of the Bible must not be underestimated—before the first century of Christianity, belief in many gods (polytheism) was common on every populated continent of the world. Why would man invent the idea of "God" anyway, if he never had any spiritual contact with God? Why would he invent the spiritual, if there were no spiritual world in the first place?

If man is just a very intelligent animal, as some scientists believe, how did he develop his highly spiritual side—which is not characteristic of any other animal? Why is it that our nearest "cousins" (chimpanzees, apes or whatever) are no more religious than our distant ones (like dogs, cats and goldfish)? Could it not be that God revealed himself to men, and that is why so many believe he exists? I'm not convinced man would figure out that there is a God through looking at nature, but I am certain that a look at nature greatly strengthens our belief in the existence of God once we accept he's there. (This seems to be Paul's argument in Romans 1.)

As human society developed, belief in one supreme God gave way to belief in many inferior gods or finally, belief in no God at all. God, however, was not man's idea. In the distant past he revealed his existence to man; God spoke.

Spiritual experience is so widespread that it presents a serious problem for materialists and atheists who deny God and the spiritual world.

PHILOSOPHY

I will spare the reader the tedium of wading through philosophical arguments: the metaphysical argument, the moral argument, the ontological argument, the teleological argument, the epistemological argument. (That would be a book in itself!) There are plenty of books you can read on these philosophical approaches to the existence of God, and most of them are helpful. Although none of them "proves" that there must be a God, they all highlight the deep difficulties of atheism.

THE BEGINNING OF THE UNIVERSE

One of the simplest and most convincing indications of the existence of a supreme being is the investigation of the origin of the universe.

Three questions must be asked:

1) Did the universe have a beginning or not?
2) Is the universe caused or uncaused?
3) Was that beginning personal or impersonal?

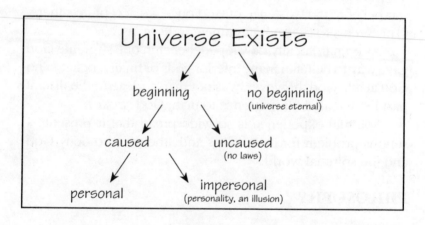

Beginning: Let us start with the fact of the existence of the universe. (I am aware that there are some philosophers who question the existence of the universe or reality itself, but we do not have time to discuss the obvious.) The universe had a definite beginning, according to scientists. The universe has been expanding as a result of a massive explosion between 10 and 20 billion years ago, according to the calculations of cosmologists and astrophysicists. Before that time, matter and energy existed in one super-condensed mass. Before this definite beginning point, there was no universe.

Someone might argue that the universe has always existed. But if that were the case, the universe would have wound down, or "stopped ticking," long ago. Like any other machine, according to the laws of physics (entropy), the universe cannot run forever; it would need maintenance, new parts, and a qualified mechanic to keep it in working order. Without the "Mechanic" the whole system would run down in a matter of time (what scientists call "heat death"). Thus we see that it simply is not possible that the physical world has always been. Science and the Bible are agreed that the world has been in existence for a limited time only.

Cause: If the universe was caused, then there must have been a cause. If it was uncaused, then it just "happened," and there was no cause. Which was the case? (Remember the watch?) The evidence we see in our world points to physical law, order and direction. Everything fits into the overall system in a remarkable way. Scientists proceed on the assumption that there is order in the world, that the observations they have made at one time and place are useful for understanding other situations as well. If there were no law and order in the physical world, there would be no science. Since the world is orderly (it can be described by physical laws), how could this order have just "happened" if, before the order, there was no law or order? If order came from non-order, or disorder, surely there was a force acting on the non-ordered material to bring the ordered world into existence. It is that simple. The universe must have been caused.

Personality: We have established that the world had a beginning and that this beginning was caused. But how do we account for the elements of personality that we see in the world today? I mean things like love and hate, reason and reflection, music, art, worship, and philosophy? What could have made impersonal matter or molecules take on a personal nature? If there is no spiritual, or non-physical, part of the universe, where did personality—non-physical characteristics in human beings—come from? Clearly there must have been some element of a personality present at the beginning. Thus the universe had a personal beginning.

Conclusion: We have reasoned that the universe had a personal, caused beginning. This cause was obviously incredibly powerful, logical, and personal, to account for what we observe today. Most people call this first cause "God." (In all fairness, however, it must be said that this argument doesn't tell us whether there is one God or many, or how powerful he is, or even whether he is good or evil.)

The argument proves the existence of God, and suggests that the God of the Bible is the one who created the universe. One thing is certain: the atheist, who claims that the world's origin and existence can be explained without any reference to God, is ignoring the evidence.

EXPERIENCE

Someone saying, "I believe in God, it feels good, so you should believe in God too," is perhaps the least convincing argument. After all, people claim religious experience in every religion of the world. But if by experience we mean that God's system works, and that happier, more productive and more fulfilling lives result when we put God's wisdom into practice, experience can be one of the strongest and most conclusive arguments for the reality of God. There is a significant difference between the lives of those who are living for God and the lives of those who do not have hope. Faith in God makes men better men, if they live consistently with that faith.

God can be experienced. But which God? What is he like? And exactly what do we mean by God? We must take this up in the next chapter.

CONCLUSION

Is anyone at home? Yes, there is a God at home in the universe. He is still there, and he has not left us without evidence of his existence. The entrance of his Son into history and the record of the Bible provide proof even more convincing than the reasons we have studied in this chapter. We will soon explore what is meant by the "Son of God" and the "Word of God" (Chapters 4 and 5). Before we do that, however, we need to sharpen our picture of God himself.

CHAPTER THREE

God: Sleeping, Retired or Dead?

The Personality of God

At noon Elijah began to taunt them. "Shout louder!" he said. "Surely he is a god! Perhaps he is deep in thought, or busy, or traveling. Maybe he is sleeping and must be awakened."

– 1 Kings 18:27

NOW THAT WE HAVE SEEN THAT IS REASONABLE THAT GOD EXISTS, we need to define our terms. What is meant by "God"? Elijah, a prophet of God in the 9th century B.C., playfully challenged the worshippers of Baal about their concept of God. They had a very human conception of God: he slept, traveled, and had a limited ability to concentrate. Sometimes we make the same mistake that the Baal-worshippers made, assuming God is limited like us. As we shall see, the most reasonable concept of God is quite different to the traditional concept of him.

It is crucial that we have an accurate concept of God. Let's not just assume everyone knows what you mean when you use the word "God." In fact, no atheist has a clear picture of who God is! The atheist's concept of God is very different from the Christian's concept, and in discussions I have found again and again that the atheist and I mean completely different things by "God."

In this chapter we will examine a number of inadequate conceptions of God, and then show that the description of God in the Bible is both true and reasonable.

INFERIOR CONCEPTS

I. The Human God

Many people speak of God in a way that implies that he is human, or no more than superhuman. People show this concept of God with questions like: "How old is God? Is he male or female? What color skin does he have?" God is

traditionally portrayed as an old man in the sky, with a long flowing robe and a great white beard. He is very lonely up there in heaven, but can be cheered up if we will take some time to remember him or say a prayer to him which soothes his loneliness and insecurity. In the old days, he used to get out more, visit the earth and perform miracles. But these days, as his health is declining, he can't get out as much. (In fact, several centuries ago rockers were installed on his celestial throne!) Anyway, this is the sort of God most of us were led to visualize, partly as a result of the representations of artists. This is what I mean by the "Human God."

In school most of us studied the ancient Greek and Roman gods: violent, drunk, lusting and having affairs, playing tricks on men. (Maybe we would behave that way if we were all-powerful—who knows?—but that doesn't mean God is like that.) Similarly, the Norse and Celtic gods (ancient northern Europe) were human in their antics. Even today, the gods of Hinduism (Indian), Buddhism and Taoism (Chinese) are seen as having cruel tendencies, sexual desires, et cetera. Most religions, both past and present, picture God as somehow human, and the "Old Man in the Sky" concept is still amazingly common in the 20th century.

Another related notion is that God is "dead." This too is based on a false concept of God, since it assumes that God ages, grows weak and loses control of his life. The German philosopher Nietzsche is famous for saying, "God is dead." I once saw the following graffiti:

GOD IS DEAD —Nietzsche.
NIETZSCHE IS DEAD —God.

Maybe your god is like the ancient Roman gods, maybe he is more of a gentlemen. Perhaps he is absent, absentminded or even dead. Either way, chances are that the "God" we have been brought up with is more human than divine. The concept is inadequate, and must be discarded.

II. I am God

Many men and women, having been influenced by eastern religions, claim that God is everywhere (true) and everything (false). Since God is identical with the universe and everything that exists must therefore be God, they claim that they are God. If this is true, then obviously everything we say must be true, since we are God. Furthermore, we created the universe, and control natural laws. Does this make any sense to you?

III. "The Force"

Influenced by the popular science fiction Star Wars films, many people, though unwilling to agree that there is a God, do acknowledge some sort of "force" in the universe. Star Wars promoted the idea that the supreme being (?) in the universe is "The Force," an all-powerful and omnipresent spiritual energy source with both a good and a bad (dark) side.

At first the "Force" concept of God sounds more scientific (and acceptable) than the traditional (Human) concept, but when we really think about it, the Force theory seems even less likely. Although forces (like electricity, flowing water, magnetism or gravity) are useful if controlled, since when do they create new life forms, increased complexity or natural laws? They don't. Any uncontrolled force (lightning, flood, tornado) is frighteningly unpredictable, and can cause electrocution, erosion and collision. Loose forces are certainly not the creator of law, order and personality. The "Force" theory explains nothing, but instead makes the origin of the world and the explanation of spiritual ideas even more of a mystery. Let us discard this idea; it too is inadequate.

IV. The Nice Warm Feeling

I have heard some people say, "I can't define God, but I feel him. When I feel at peace and happy, and have that nice warm feeling in my tummy—that's God." It seems such people are getting truth confused with their feelings about truth. Yes, we may feel nice when we are convinced there is a God—but we may also feel nice after a delicious dinner or a refreshing swim in the ocean. Any idea of God which reduces him to the level of a hot meal or a cold shower certainly misses the whole point. That sort of notion, though it may feel nice, explains nothing, and answers none of the important questions about God and the universe. This idea too must be discarded.

V. Idolatry

Billions of people in the world worship idols—statues of gods which they believe are somehow linked with the gods themselves. Idolatry (idol worship) is widespread, even in traditional Christendom. One basic error of idolatry is that it breeds a physical conception of God instead of a spiritual understanding. Another serious error is that it encourages us to manipulate God: we present offerings to the statue or picture, and the god is somehow obligated to answer our prayer. We offer the idol some special food, paper, money, incense, or even a prayer, and we think that the blessing is ours. Instead of God controlling us, we control God. This is the serious error of idolatry. As the early Christian leader Paul said to the idolatrous residents of Athens:

> The God who made the world and everything in it is the
> Lord of heaven and earth and does not live in temples
> built by hands. And he is not served by human hands, as if
> he needed anything, because he himself gives all men life
> and breath and everything else (Acts 17:24-25).

VI. Modern Idolatry

Many in the western world do not worship religious idols, yet, they do make "idols" of other people, fine cars, stereo systems, money, sex, leisure, education, etc. On top of all this, their concept of God is idolatrous, too.

The basic error of idolatry is that we put ourselves in the place of God. Instead of him controlling us, we control him (or try to).

In modern society we often try to control God. Times of trouble come, and we become extra religious. (Once I was nearly killed by a car, and I quickly became sober and spiritual—for two weeks!) Sometimes we feel a special need for God in the time of sickness, financial difficulty, the death of a friend, or uncertainty about the future.

We use God as a "crutch." When the trouble is past, we abandon him. He is there whenever we need him. (In the Bible we learn that we are to be there whenever he needs us!) This is modern idolatry. Its approach to God must be abandoned if we are to ever understand who God really is.

VII. Ask No Questions!

This is the attitude of many towards discussions about God. They are happy for you to believe (or disbelieve) in God, and they don't care whether or not your concept of God agrees with their concept of God. "After all," they reason, "it's all the same God, whatever you call it. What does it really matter?" This is the ultimate flexible God. He is whatever you want him to be. As long as the word "God" is used, everyone is happy and no one asks any questions. But whether done deliberately or not, this is clearly an attempt to avoid learning the truth about God.

As a whole, mankind has been unwilling to grasp God in a reasonable way. God created us in his image, but we have "recreated" God in our image. Has your concept of God been any of the above?

THE REASONABLE CONCEPT

Beyond Space and Time

Attempts to limit God to a particular location or time are bound to fail, because God is beyond space and time. Physicists, following the mathematical insights of Einstein, have proven that space and time form a "continuum." You do not have to be an Einstein to realize the implications of this: anything or anyone outside of our universe must be outside of time. God is outside our universe, so he is not limited by time. He has all eternity to listen to the split-second prayer of a pilot as he goes down in the flames. He views our lives from beginning to end spread out before him like a sheet of paper, and it is no challenge for him to work all things together to answer our prayers. Since he is not limited by space, he can be in all places at the same time, and is at work in the lives of every human being in the world simultaneously.

Twentieth-century physicists have made some astounding discoveries. But the insights they have devoted whole lifetimes to acquiring have been clearly laid out in the Bible for 2,000 years:

God is spirit...(John 4:24).

For in him we live and move and have our being...(Acts 17:28).

...to him all are alive (Luke 20:38).

...With the Lord a day is like a thousand years, and a thousand years are like a day (2 Peter 3:8).

What does this mean?

- God is spiritual, not physical. He is not part of the physical world.

- God is everywhere at all times.

- God is timeless, not limited by time.

Flatland, an imaginative book written in the last century by an Oxford mathematician, describes the adventures of "A Square" (a man in Flatland, a two-dimensional world which existed in a plane) as he tries to understand the three-dimensional world, and such beings as cubes and spheres. Although the book is a mathematical adventure and not a religious book, there are valuable spiritual applications.

One day the world of the square (Flatland) is invaded by a sphere (a ball, or three-dimensional circle). At first the

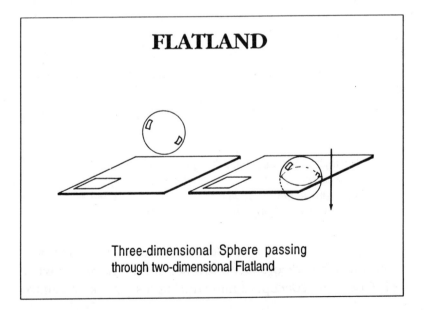

FLATLAND

Three-dimensional Sphere passing through two-dimensional Flatland

square sees only a point, then a circle, but soon the circle grows larger and larger. This is extremely frustrating to the square, to whom it seems that natural laws are being broken. Nothing becomes something! (The sphere, or the edge of the sphere, appears from nowhere.) That something grows, becomes quite large, and then starts to shrink. (The sphere is passing through the plane and every time the square takes a look, he sees a cross-section of the sphere, which is a circle.) Eventually, the sphere vanishes completely. What a mystery!

The sphere tries to communicate with the square, to help the square to understand his nature. But the square cannot comprehend a three-dimensional circle (a sphere), only a normal two-dimensional circle. It is not until the bewildered square travels to a three-dimensional world that he is even willing to believe that three-dimensional circles could exist. Finally the square is made a believer, and returns to Flatland, but he is unable to convince his family and fellow citizens, who decide that he is crazy, and have him imprisoned.

Since God exists in a higher dimension than our own, we have only the faintest inkling of his nature. Understanding him fully would be as difficult for us as it was for the square to comprehend the sphere. We may see various facets or cross-sections of him as he acts in the world, and we can certainly see the effects of his activity, but there can be no complete knowledge of him. Similarly, the Bible teaches that God's ways are far above our ways:

> "For my thoughts are not your thoughts, neither are your ways my ways," declares the Lord. "As the heavens are higher than the earth, so are my ways higher than your ways and my thoughts than your thoughts" (Isaiah 55:8-9).

As the Bible teaches and science indicates, God is above or outside our world of space and time. That is one reason why he is God. Any concept of him which does not take this into account is woefully inadequate. That God is beyond space and time is reasonable. It's amazing how many non-believers prefer to attack the "Old Man in the Sky" idea!

Personal but not Human

As long as we insist on making God human, or "making him in our own image," we are bound to attribute our weaknesses to God. In other words, a humanistic concept of God will lead us to imagine he has selfish motives for what he says and does, is blind to many of our actions and thoughts, is forgetful and inconsistent in his standards. If God were just a superhuman, this might be true, but he isn't, as we have shown. This is exactly in accordance with what the Scriptures teach:

> God is not a man, that he should lie...
> (Numbers 23:19).
>
> ...God is love (1 John 4:8).
>
> Your eyes are too pure to look on evil; you cannot
> tolerate wrong (Habakkuk 1:13).

What does this mean:

- God is not human; he has no human weakness.
- God is good; his love is constant. The purpose he has for our lives is good as well, and we should seek to discover it and live by it.
- He is sinless, and cannot compromise his character by tolerating evil.

Once again we see that the biblical concept of God is both true and reasonable. We all need to adjust our conception of God to match the biblical concept. Although he loves us, and

41

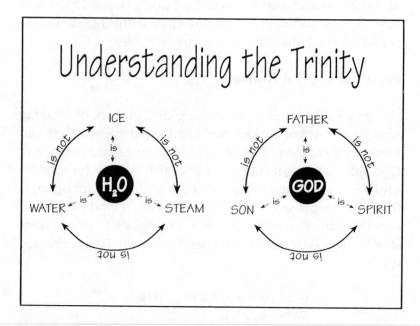

whatever good qualities we have come from him, he does not share our weaknesses.

One comment on the love of God: how could God love if he has always existed, even when there was no one else to love? Was God really lonely? Is that why he created man? No, for although he created man in order to love him, God already was loving. Christians believe that the one God is composed of three persons, called the trinity. As you can see from the diagram above, God is Father, Son and Spirit but all three are God in nature. It is a difficult teaching to understand, but it explains beautifully how love existed in God eternally.

If this is hard to understand, consider the three forms of water: ice (solid), steam (gas), and water (liquid). Ice = water, and steam = water, but it's not true to say that ice = steam. So it is with the trinity.

Spiritual not Physical

The teaching of the Bible that God created man in his own "image" (Genesis 1:27) has been totally misunderstood. God did not create man in his physical image (after all, God is spiritual, not physical), but rather in his spiritual image. We love, reflect, have free will and spiritual values, contemplate the universe and eternity, et cetera, this is what it means to be created in the image of God.

An accurate picture of God must take into account that he is a spiritual being, not a physical one. Let us again read what the Bible says:

> God is spirit...(John 4:24).

> Where can I go from your Spirit? Where can I flee from your presence? (Psalm 139:7).

> ...God is light...(1 John 1:5).

> ...The heavens, even the highest heaven, cannot contain you. How much less this temple I have built! (1 Kings 8:27).

And what does this mean?

- God is a spiritual being. The word spiritual does not mean unreal or make-believe, only non-physical.
- Because God is Spirit, he can exist in all places at all times.
- God brings spiritual light into our hearts, and helps us to see spiritually.
- God is not some spirit or vapor that can be trapped and forced into a box (remember Ghost Busters?).

43

This concept of God makes sense; it's reasonable. The biblical idea of God is found nowhere else than in the Bible. This concept of God is taught by no other world religion, and yet it squares perfectly with scientific principles and common sense.

SLEEPING, RETIRED OR DEAD?

No, God is not sleeping, retired or dead. He is awake, active and very much alive! But we must have some idea of what we are looking for if we are to recognize him. Unfortunately, all of us have had a distorted view of who God is, and have failed to recognize him because of these misconceptions. Fortunately, God can be understood, and what we can understand makes sense. Moreover, his nature is revealed perfectly in the character of Jesus Christ, as we'll see in the next chapter.

CHAPTER FOUR

Jesus: "*Good Moral Teacher*"?

The Son of God

W ISE RABBI," ONE MAN SAID. "YES, A GREAT TEACHER, PERHAPS the greatest that ever lived," said another. "A good moral teacher, that's what he was," chimed in yet another. Thus they spoke about Jesus of Nazareth, the carpenter from a small village in first-century Israel. And all of them completely mistaken!

We must come to grips with the fact that Jesus of Nazareth was not just a "good moral teacher." He may have been many things, but that he was a good moral teacher is highly unlikely! What did he claim about himself? And how can we evaluate those claims? These are the questions we will address in this chapter.

PERSPECTIVE: THE INCARNATION

Since God exists, it is reasonable that he speaks, that he is not a silent God. This will be demonstrated at length in the next chapter, where we will explore what is meant by the "Word of God". But there is another way that God has communicated to us, the most personal communication possible: the Incarnation.

The term incarnation simply means God becoming flesh, or human. God became man, in Jesus Christ, the Son of God. That is the incarnation, the most profound miracle of all history. It all sounds quite theological, so perhaps an illustration will help.

Imagine a colony of ants, busily going about their business, completely unaware that a hungry anteater is approaching. A scientist comes across the unsuspecting colony, and wishing to warn them of the danger, tries shouting at them; that does not work. He then tries pointing the way to safety with his finger; that too fails. Finally he comes up with an ingenious idea, a radical idea: he himself will become an ant! Somehow, drawing on all his scientific ability, he transforms himself into an ant—now he can speak to them in their language, show them the way to safety, and rescue them from death. That is more or less what God did in Jesus: he came down to our level.

It might be asked why the scientist would concern himself with the ants, and even more why the Lord of the universe would concern himself with the earth, the lost planet, spinning its way to destruction. That is an excellent question; fortunately for us, God is a God of love, and through Jesus we can personally know his love. Jesus chose to come to earth, to share in all the blood, toil, tears and sweat of human existence. Yet Jesus did not come only to inform us, but to give us a personal knowledge of God, through dying for our sins so that we could draw near to the holy God.

> ...the Word was God...The Word became flesh and made his dwelling among us. We have seen his glory, the glory of the One and Only, who came from the Father...No one has ever seen God, but God the One and Only, who is at the Father's side, has made him known (John 1:1, 14, 18).

This is the perspective necessary for understanding Jesus and his claims.

THE RADICAL CLAIMS OF CHRIST

Consider only twenty-four of the incredible claims that Jesus Christ made about himself. (I have reworded them slightly, but if you check the references you will see that they are correct.)

CLAIMS OF JESUS CHRIST

I have always existed ....John 8:58, 17:5
I hold the keys to death ....Revelation 1:18
I have never sinned ....John 8:46
I have all authority on heaven and earth ..Matthew 28:18
I and the Father are one ....John 10:30
I must be placed above your family ....Matthew 10:37
I have authority to forgive sins ....Mark 2:7-10
I am the light of the world ....John 8:12
I am prophesied in the Scriptures ....Luke 24:25-27
I am from heaven ....John 8:23
I will be resurrected ....Mark 8:31
I am the bread of life ....John 6:35
I will send the Spirit of God Almighty ....John 16:7
I am coming again to the earth ....Revelation 22:20
I am a king ....John 18:37
I give spiritual life ....John 5:24
I am the one through whom you must pray ...John 16:23-24
I heal diseases ....Luke 13:32
I will judge the world on Judgment Day ......John 5:22-30
I am the Son of God ....Matthew 16:16-17
I will raise the dead at the end of time ....John 5:28-29
I am the only way to God—no exceptions........John 14:6
My words will never pass away ....Matthew 24:35
If you reject me, you reject God himself.........Luke 10:16

Yes, these are astounding claims! (And they are either true or false; there is no middle ground.) No religious leader before

47

or since has ever dared to make such claims! (Have you ever known a good moral teacher who has claimed to be sinless, to be God, or to have always existed?) The assessment of C. S. Lewis, who became a believer on considering the evidence, is to the point:

> A man who was merely a man and said the sort of things Jesus said would not be a great moral teacher. He would either be a lunatic—on a level with the man who says he is a poached egg—or else he would be the Devil of hell. You must make your choice. Either he was, and is, the Son of God: or else a madman or something worse. You can shut Him up for a fool; you can spit at Him and kill Him as a demon; or you can fall at his feet and call him Lord and God. But let us not come with any patronizing nonsense about him being a great human teacher. He has not left that open to us. He did not intend to. *Mere Christianity, II.3.52*

A number of evidences books, following Lewis' reasoning, have shown convincingly that Jesus was exactly who he claimed to be. There are several ways to interpret these claims. Let's examine them and see which is most reasonable.

LEGEND, LIAR, LUNATIC, OR LORD?

The Bible is the proper starting place for any evaluation of Jesus' claims, since that is the best source for what he said, as well as how he lived. So we begin with the Christ of the Bible. There are only four possibilities:

(1) **LEGEND.** Some deny that Jesus ever existed or made those claims; they treat Jesus as Legend. (Very few people really believe this, but we will consider the possibility anyway.)

(2) **LIAR.** Now if he was not merely a legend—if the Jesus of the Bible really existed—there are only two options: either he spoke the truth or he did not. If he did not speak the truth and knew it, he was a Liar.

(3) **LUNATIC.** If, on the other hand, Jesus thought he was speaking the truth—even though he wasn't—he would by definition be quite insane, hence a Lunatic.

(4) **LORD.** Think about it; if the above three possibilities can be ruled out, there remains only one alternative: that he spoke the truth, and is who he claimed to be.

THE INESCAPABLE VERDICT

Legend: The Legend view is represented by the noted atheist Bertrand Russell, who once said in a lecture:

> Historically it is quite doubtful whether Christ ever existed at all, and if he did we do not know anything about him...*Why I Am Not A Christian, 6 March 1927.*

On the contrary, it is certain that Christ existed. His enemies certainly admitted his existence! Christ is referred to by first-century Roman and Jewish historians (Tacitus, Suetonius, Thallus, and Josephus, to mention only a few). Archaeology has shown that the four biographies, or gospels, of Jesus' life were written in the lifetime of his contemporaries. But legends usually take many generations, if not centuries, to build up and circulate. The gap between original events and the recording of them is simply too narrow.

To think that the early Christians created the character "Christ," or put words into his mouth that he never spoke, is ridiculous. That would be like a strange new religious sect springing up which claimed that Winston Churchill is God, performed miracles, and rose from the dead! Who would believe it? There are too many eyewitnesses to the contrary, and Churchill died too recently. Early Christian leaders like Peter and Paul knew the difference between true life and legend (2 Peter 1:16). Further, they refused to put words into Jesus' mouth (1 Corinthians 7:12). Both these men died for their faith in Jesus Christ. And if the early Christians were in the habit of making up miracle stories about their heroes, why does the Bible say that John the Baptist, a very influential and powerful figure, never did even one miracle (John 10:41)?

Bertrand Russell is wrong not only about the existence of Christ, but also about what can be known about him. Although most of the historical material on Jesus is found in the Bible (where you would naturally expect to find it!), there are many other writers who mentioned him, as we have noted. In addition, his character and teachings were reproduced in his followers' lives!

Lastly, would a legend have had such a tremendous impact on our planet as Jesus has had? Legends may make entertaining reading, but do they inspire men and women to die for them? Do they lead to urgent missionary activity, social concern, and changed lives? There is no other person in history who has had such an impact on the world as Jesus Christ! The "Legend" suggestion must be ruled out; it explains nothing and ignores all the evidence.

Liar: Jesus existed, so we must move on to consider the three remaining possibilities. He made incredible claims. Perhaps they were lies, and Jesus knew all along that they were lies, but is it really conceivable that Jesus, whom even unbelievers generally concede was a man of truth and integrity, was a liar? It is likely that a man known for his emphasis on truthfulness would be a liar himself? Or that he would send many of his followers to their deaths as they preached the message about him which he knew was sheer fabrication? Is it even remotely likely that a man whose life was consumed with exposing religious hypocrisy would be the greatest hypocrite of all, a master deceiver? No, it is not.

And what would the motive be for this deceit? Personal curiosity about crucifixion? Money? Jesus, who taught "It is more blessed to give than to receive" (Acts 20:35), died penniless. Hatred for humanity? Then why would he die for the sins of the world, including his enemies? There was no motive in Jesus' life for lying. Common sense tells us that it is more likely that he never existed at all than that he was a liar!

Lunatic: Still assuming that what Jesus said was untrue, but now withdrawing the charge of deceit, it follows that he must have been a lunatic. No man could have been made the extraordinary claims Jesus made and believed them if he were not insane. But when we look at the character of Jesus what do we see? The imbalanced personality of a madman? No, we see perfect balance.

Jesus was tender and loving, but not sentimental; zealous and fearless, but wise and cautious; unworldly, but not antisocial; confident, but not arrogant; self-sacrificing, yet still joyful; urgent and responsible, but peaceful and unhurried; often under attack, but always composed and never rattled; strong and uncompromising, but not harsh; a man of dignity and authority, but still humble; a powerful leader, and yet a man of prayer and a servant of servants. Was Jesus unstable? Hardly!

In short, Jesus' personality shows none of the instability, obsession, irrational fears, paranoia, anxiety, mood swings or introversion that we would expect in a lunatic. Jesus is so perfectly balanced, in fact, that he is the standard for sanity.

Lord: There is only one remaining option: he is Lord, as his disciples believe and teach. What he said was true, and he knew it was true. Jesus Christ was not some legend and certainly not a liar or lunatic. He spoke the truth; every one of his claims is true. (Go back and read them again!)

To say Jesus was just a "good moral teacher" is like saying that Albert Einstein was a good mathematician. Einstein was most certainly not a good mathematician; he was great, as everyone admits! Similarly, Jesus Christ is not just a good moral teacher; he is God, and truth itself.

The verdict is inescapable: Jesus Christ is Lord.

THE ULTIMATE CLAIM

Jesus, as we have shown, was far more than just a good moral teacher. Anyone who asserts that this is all he was is either totally unaware of his claims, or has forgotten them through weakness of memory. The crux of the matter is that Jesus Christ, the Son of God, died on the cross for our sins.

The little boy was playing on the railroad tracks, unknown to his father. By the time the father noticed him it was too late: he looked with horror as he saw the two passenger trains speeding towards each other from different directions; they were on a collision course! The only way to prevent the collision was to re-direct one of the trains off onto another track, exactly where his son was playing. The father had to act fast—it was only seconds before the collision—but he loved his son! What would he do?

He threw the switch, saved the passengers, but in doing so sacrificed his little boy's life.

God threw the switch for us. It was the only way to save us. He watched his son die for our sins. Yet most of the world carries on along its selfish course, unaware and unappreciative of the sacrifice that God made for us!

What is the ultimate claim? It is the claim that Jesus Christ, by virtue of his death, has on your life.

What is your response?

CHAPTER FIVE

The Bible:
The "Good Book"?

The Authority of the Word of God

"What is truth?"
—Pontius Pilate

S UCH WERE THE WORDS OF PONTIUS PILATE, THE ROMAN governor who authorized the crucifixion of the Son of God around 33 A. D. Not just Pilate, but the entire world of his day was confused about truth. And not just the first-century world, but our entire 20th-century world is hopelessly confused about the truth. Many ask the question, "What is truth?", but few have any answers.

"Truth" these days is a sensitive subject, one over which people are easily offended. This is especially the case in politics (Is war ever justified? Is socialism the best system?) and ethical issues (Is smoking marijuana necessarily wrong? How about abortion?)—areas which affect us personally.

Let's consider some areas less likely to stir the emotions, like mathematics: what is 3 x 4? One man may say 10, another 12, and another might even say 13. But should those who said 10 and 13 be offended when we point out to them their mistake? Of course not! Or take the field of chemistry: Nitrous oxide (N_2O), known as laughing gas, is used by doctors and dentists as an anesthetic. Nitric oxide (NO), on the other hand, is a deadly poison. Or is it the other way around? The answer to the question matters a lot, and hopefully it would not take a terrible accident to make it clear which one is safe and which is the poison!

People are often offended when others express their religious view, but why should they be? Just as in mathematics and chemistry, there are right and wrong answers to the basic questions of life: Is there a God? Why do I exist? Does God care about me? What is my purpose in life? How can I change? Is there life after death?

THE UNRELIABILITY OF FEELINGS

Unfortunately, most people make their decisions about truth based on their own convenience or their feelings. But feelings are an extremely unreliable means of discerning the truth; they change like the weather. Some days we feel more spiritual, sacrificial or selfless than others. What does not feel right one day may feel fine the next. Even our feelings about spiritual truth can change—and often do! Feelings are simply too subjective! We cannot know the truth through our feelings.

What we need is an objective standard—something which is consistent, based on truth itself and not on changing human emotions.

THE SILENT GOD?

Many people grant that there may be a God, but scoff at the idea that he would speak to man. He is the Silent God, one who never speaks. They picture him as having wound up the universe many eons ago and then left it to run, a sort of a heavenly clockmaker. Now he has lost contact with his creation, and claims of his speaking to men are merely wishful thinking. But is this reasonable? If God exists, could he not speak? (Of course he could!) And if he could speak, would he not communicate to men, whom he created? (Naturally!) Indeed, why would God go to all the trouble of creating the world and mankind, then to break off contact with him? What would be the point of that? As for those who claim God does speak to us, but only through nature or our feelings, we must question how much we can really learn about God from nature—or human nature! Once we accept sunsets, breezes, shivers and feelings of joy as messages from God, anything goes! Your guess is as good as mine; who is to say what the truth is? Again, we need an objective standard! If there is a God (and there is) and if there is truth (which there also is), then it makes perfect sense that God himself is the one who tells us what truth is. Away, then, with this notion of the "Silent God"!

GOD'S MESSAGE TO MAN

Once we have come to grips with the fact that God can and in all probability does speak to men, we are ready to consider what sort of message God would provide. We would expect the message to be:

VERBAL: Since men think in words, the message from God to man must be in words—a verbal message. Feelings change, but words are a constant.

INTELLIGIBLE: It must be capable of being understood, not mysterious like hieroglyphs or vague like a horoscope. (What sort of god would he be who was unable to express himself clearly?) Furthermore, it must be intelligible to all mankind, not only to the educated or those sharing one particular culture.

CONSISTENT: The message from God should not be confused. You would not expect it to contradict the proven facts of science, history, archaeology, logic, et cetera.

Moreover, the message of the Bible does not contradict itself. (In Chapter 7 we will address the issue of supposed "contradictions.")

AUTHORITATIVE: The Bible presents itself over and over as the ultimate message from God to men in every nation of the world. Writers and speakers in the Bible do not apologize for their bold statement of truth; they expect their audience to accept it and change!

SUPERNATURAL: The Bible shows all the signs of being the supernatural book mentioned above. Consider the fulfilled prophesies alone: some accurately predict the rise and fall of nations, others announce the coming of the Messiah (Christ, or "anointed one"). For example, Micah 5, Isaiah 53 and other passages foretell the birth and saving death of Jesus in remarkable detail—hundreds of years before the event!

PRACTICAL: Yes, it does work! Millions of men and women the world over are living proof of the fact.

This is what Christians mean when they speak of the Bible as "the Word of God." It is God's message from heaven to us. No other religious writings in the world even come close to supporting this claim. (The entire second section of this book is devoted to demonstrating the uniqueness of the Bible.)

THE BIBLE: DEFINITION

What exactly is the "Bible"? It is the written revelation from God to man, revealed to at least 50 men during a period of over a thousand years. The Bible comprises 66 parts, called "books": 39 books in the Old Testament, 27 in the New Testament. The Old Testament was revealed to men before the time of Jesus, the New Testament during and after his lifetime.

Each book is divided into chapters, and if you read three or four chapters a day it is possible to read the entire Bible in a year. Yet very few have ever read the entire Bible; they do not truly believe (or understand) that it is God's authoritative, inspired message to man. If you are investigating Christianity for the first time, begin with the Bible.

THE "GOOD BOOK"?

Often we hear people casually refer to the Bible as "the good book." By this they don't necessarily mean that it is their favorite book, or that they seriously try to put it into practice in their daily lives. What they mean is that it is a good book, and they respect the conviction of those who believe it is actually God's book from himself to man.

Now either the Bible is God's book to man or it is not. If it is not, fair enough. But if it is, the weak tribute paid to it as "good literature" or "the good book" simply will not do. If it is God's message, it is not only a good book, but in one sense the only (completely) good book!

This claim, if true, has serious and far-reaching consequences. If this is true, have you read it? I don't mean, have you looked through parts of it, as a schoolchild might do. I mean, have you seriously examined the Bible? For if God has spoken to man, it would be a tragedy not to hear his voice.

CONCLUSION

Now, back to Pilate's question, "What is truth?" To answer it, there are two urgent things we must do:

- Start reading God's Word, the Bible.
- Be willing to obey the Bible.

Jesus said, in his prayer to God on the night before his execution, "Your word is truth" (John 17:17). Jesus knew that we must turn to God to find the truth, and that the truth is the Word of God. That is why we must read the Bible.

He also said, "If you hold to my teaching, you are really my disciples. Then you will know the truth, and the truth will set you free" (John 8:31-32). Jesus is saying that we cannot truly understand the truth unless we are willing to follow the truth— wherever it leads! And in John 7:17 he said, "If anyone chooses to do God's will, he will find out whether my teaching comes from God..." That is why we must be willing to do God's will. If we are unwilling, then even when we stare the truth in the face we will be unable to recognize it.

We have seen that it is completely reasonable that there is a God, and that he speaks. He speaks to us not in a subjective way (our feelings or opinions), but in an objective way.

Christians recognize that this objective communication from God to man is found in the Bible, a book unique among all religious writings. But the Bible is not a "good book." It is the Word of God!

THE BIBLE

In Section I many introductory matters were covered, and we demonstrated that it is completely reasonable that God exists that Jesus Christ—by virtue of his life, claims and death—is the Son of God, and that the Bible is just the sort of communication we would expect from God to man. Indeed, "He is there and he is not silent!" In the four chapters of Section II we will examine the reliability of the Bible, how its teaching compares with other major world religions, and finally the question of miracles in the Bible, particularly the resurrection of Jesus Christ from the dead.

CHAPTER SIX

Can We Take God at His Word?

The Reliability of the Bible

OFTEN IT IS CONFIDENTLY ASSERTED THAT THE BIBLE IS NOT IN FACT the Word of God, but only the word of man. Critics state that we have no reason to trust the Bible, that what was originally said and meant by Jesus and others is long since lost to history. The aim of the following dialog is to show that this is false: the Bible is the Word of God, and God has preserved that Word faithfully for thousands of years. The conclusion, as we shall see, is that we are indeed able to take God at his word!

DEADLY RECIPE

Hans Kritic: Jacoby, my friend, I find it interesting that one as bright as you would hold everything in the Bible as the Word of God, when in fact it is just another work of men. It has some very good things in it, but I find it impossible to trust the Bible unconditionally. It is most likely that what was originally said and meant by Jesus and others is long since lost to history.

Douglas Jacoby, disciple: Mr. Kritic, if you will just give me a few minutes of your time and an open heart and mind, I can show you that the Bible is completely the Word of God, and that God has preserved that Word faithfully over the last 2,000 years. I would like for you to know why I have come to the conclusion that we are indeed able to take God at his word!

Imagine for a minute that you, Mr. Kritic, are invited to a dinner, and when the main course is served the host turns to you and says, "You're really going to enjoy this meal—it's sort of a game. Nearly every item on your plate is non-poisonous. Have a nice dinner!" What would you do? Hope the worst that could happen is indigestion, not death? Guess that it's only the mushrooms in the tossed salad that are deadly, and take your chances? Would you risk your life in order not to offend your host?

Hans: That's an interesting little riddle, Jacoby, but what's the point?

Douglas: Bear with me and I think you will see. Isn't it true, Hans (may I call you that?), that you would refuse to eat? Why play the game at all if there's no way to win? Either you must be able to trust all the ingredients in the meal, or you can trust none at all! It's all or nothing. In the same way, it's all or nothing with the Bible. Either you can trust God's Word (all of it), or you can't really trust any of it. For if some parts are in error, what reliable way would you have to sort out the bad bits? (Our own opinions and feelings are too unreliable.)

Hans: But, Jacoby, if someone is a lot more knowledgeable and experienced than I, he can still generally be trusted, even though he makes a few mistakes now and again. So why can't we just generally trust the Bible?

Douglas: Hans, that argument sounds good, but there is one important difference here. When it comes to matters of right and wrong, heaven and hell, it's just too risky—eternal issues are at stake! We need to know whether we are on the right track or not. Critics of the Bible have correctly supposed that if they could discredit one or two teachings of the Bible, faith in the Bible would become unreasonable. If the Bible is wrong, let's say, about the experience of Israel at the Red Sea, how do we know it's not wrong about the resurrection of Jesus from the dead? And if it might be wrong about that, how do we know what in the world it is right about?

61

Hans, would you agree that an infinitely powerful God could, if he chose to, communicate his Word to people?

Hans: I'll admit the whole idea sounds rather strange to me, but I suppose I would have to agree that an infinitely powerful God could do whatever he chose to do.

Douglas: Exactly, and there is no reason on earth why he could not choose to give us his Word in a book! But how could we trust in God if his Word were true sometimes, and false at other times? (How could I trust you if I never knew whether or not you were telling the truth?)

MUCH CONFUSION?

Hans: But, Jacoby, even loyal fellow that you are, you must admit that there is so much confusion about the Bible.

Douglas: Yes, but much of it is caused by people with strong opinions about the Bible, but who in many cases have hardly read it! Some of the opinions are held by religious people who give the impression that you don't have to believe the Bible (or even read it for that matter) to be a good Christian. Critics with certain impressive-sounding credentials also cause a great deal of confusion, especially when they are readily believed by people who have never studied the Bible or known a practicing Christian. There are many men in high places (clergy types) who publicly deny one of the central Christian teachings: that Jesus rose from the dead. All these people are responsible for the confusion today about God's Word, yet there is a group of people who I believe do even more harm. They are those who say, "I believe in the Bible."

Hans: I wouldn't have expected that from you, Jacoby. What on earth do you mean?

Douglas: Of course, I'm not saying that we shouldn't believe in God's Word, or tell others that we do. But these days most people who say, "I believe in the Bible" are very confused.

You may ask them, "Do you accept what Jesus said about sex before marriage?" They say:

"Well, not that part. The Bible was written so long ago, and this is the 20th century!" (As though man has really changed!)

"How about the teaching of the Scriptures on the need to attend a strong church, and to share our faith with others?"

"No, I just don't have time for all that. I have such a busy life." (As though no one else does!)

"Then you mean that you don't believe in the Bible?"

"No, I do—I believe in most all of it, except..."

"Except the parts you find inconvenient?"

"Well, yes. And also a passage or two of the Old Testament. I could never accept the story about Moses and the Ark."

"You mean Noah and the Ark?"

"OK, OK! What does it matter? All that counts is being a nice person, and I think I'm a pretty decent fellow."

Actually it matters a lot. Either we can take God at his word, or we can't. Does this person (the one who claims to believe in the Bible) really believe in the Bible? No, he believes in himself, and the Bible happens to support his opinions now and again. But whenever there is a conflict between his opinion and God's Word, he stops "believing" in the Bible. So who's the real authority: himself or God? Clearly such a person does not believe in the Bible at all.

Remember, it's all or nothing! Let's not be confused.

GOSSIP?

Hans: But Jacoby, the original documents in the Bible were written several thousand years ago. How can we be certain that our Bible today is a reliable copy of the original (Hebrew) Old Testament and (Greek) New Testament books?

Douglas: I will agree, Hans, that this question is extremely important, because if there were significant changes, the message God gave could have been lost, or seriously distorted.

How could God entrust such a vital task to humans, especially in the days before photocopiers!

Perhaps, Hans, you have played the game sometimes called "Gossip." A short message is whispered into the ear of the first person, who turns and whispers it to the next, and so on around the room. The end result can be surprisingly different from the original message; it may be much longer, and nearly always the content of the message is drastically altered.

I know that many people think of the modern Bible in the same way. They view their English translation as a translation of another language translated from another language from yet another language and so on...which may very well have been inaccurately copied from the original manuscripts. This notion is extremely common, and extremely misleading.

VARIANT READINGS

Hans: But Jacoby, you surely know that all of the manuscripts of the Bible are not identical. Have you ever noticed those little notes at the bottom of the pages in your own Bible?

Douglas: You are right, Hans, there are differences in the manuscripts. There are about 1,100 chapters in the Bible, and although copyists took great pains to avoid slips of the pen, there are thousands of "variants." Nearly all these variants are spelling mistakes, minor differences in word order (Christ Jesus instead of Jesus Christ), or instances of a copyist missing a word or line (Jesus sat down began to teach). When a manuscript has a variant, it is compared to other older manuscripts, and a decision is made about which reading is original. In over 99% of these cases, agreement among scholars is total. (When it isn't, these trivial variants are indicated in the footnotes of the Bible.) What we are saying is that the manuscript variations are completely insignificant.

The "originals" have been lost, but that is no reason to fear. The "originals" of nearly every work from ancient history have been lost—but copies have been made, for the most part by very careful copyists. Whenever there is a difference between one copy and another, historians do their very best to reconstruct the original version accurately.

Let me show you this little chart, Hans. As you can see, ancient manuscripts usually don't survive, so the oldest surviving copies tend to be much later than the original.

The Transmission of Various Ancient Manuscripts

Author	Date	Oldest Copy	Interval	Copies
Aristophanes	400 B.C.	900 A.D.	1300 years	45
Aristotle	340 B.C.	1100 A.D.	1450 years	5
Julius Caesar	50 B.C.	900 A.D.	950 years	10
Herodotus	435 B.C.	900 A.D.	1350 years	8
Plato	360 B.C.	800 A.D.	1150 years	15
Sophocles	415 B.C.	1000 A.D.	1400 years	7
Thucydides	410 B.C.	900 A.D.	1300 years	8

Despite the long intervals between the time of the original texts and the oldest surviving copies, historians do not conclude that these writings are "unreliable" or "corrupt". If we refuse to accept the reliable transmission of the Bible, we would (logically) have to reject almost everything else from ancient history! Whether or not you are familiar with the writers mentioned above, you can easily appreciate the significance of the evidence when we consider the hard facts of the Bible.

It is true that the New Testament (N.T.) is supported by more manuscripts than the Old Testament, but both are extremely well attested. (The Dead Sea Scrolls, discovered in

1947, prove the excellent transmission of the Old Testament.)
And what exactly is the evidence for the New Testament?

Look, Hans, at what I call "the hard facts."

THE HARD FACTS

- The New Testament was written approximately 50 to 100 A.D.
- The earliest fragment of a New Testament manuscript dates from 125 A.D. It is the gospel of John—written only 30 years earlier!
- Manuscripts of entire books of the New Testament date from 200 A.D.
- Thus the interval of time in this case is only 100 years!
- The oldest copy of the complete New Testament dates from 350 A.D.—a gap of only 250 years, compared with gaps of four or five times as long (1,000 years or so) for most works of classical authors.
- The gap for most Old Testament books, for comparison, is as little as 200-400 years.
- There are over 5,000 ancient Greek copies alone!
- Including ancient copies in other languages, there are well over 40,000 complete and partial manuscripts of the New Testament!
- In addition, there are well over 35,000 quotations from the N.T. in early writers, almost all of which date earlier than the oldest surviving N.T. manuscripts! Thus, even if all our N.T. manuscripts *were* lost, it would not be difficult to reconstruct most of the N.T. from these references. The Bible is by far the best attested book from ancient times! No other classical work even comes close.

The facts are impressive indeed. As we have seen, there
is no reason whatsoever to doubt the reliability of the Biblical
text as it has been passed down.

His Word today is the same message that was preached
thousands of years ago, and it is just as relevant now as then.

Hans: But, Jacoby, you Christians aren't the only people who have scriptures. There are many other religions in the world that have their own and are just as devoted to them.

Douglas: First, Hans, I'm not sure how devoted some people are to their scriptures. In many religions their scriptures are seldom read, left instead for the "experts."

But, secondly, there are some major differences between the Bible and the scriptures of other world religions. Let me list a few:

Conciseness: The Bible packs an amazing amount into a few pages. Eastern scriptures, on the other hand, are so extensive that it would take the average person several lifetimes to read the scriptures of his religion. In Buddhism, for example, the scriptures are thousands of times longer than the Christian Bible. (No wonder scripture is played down!) The Hindu creation story is hundreds of pages long, whereas the Bible puts the creation into just a few verses. In addition, most of the Bible is easy to follow, whereas Muslim, Hindu and especially Buddhist scriptures contain enormous numbers of obscure verses which even their top theologians cannot explain. Finally, many religions have very complicated laws and rituals outside their scriptures. Biblical Christianity fits all its teaching within the pages of one Bible. We trust a concise speaker more readily than a rambling one—he is trying to make his point clear, not confuse, impress or cloud the issues.

Purity: From my reading of the Koran, Upanishads, Bhagavad Gita, Sutras, Analects of Confucius, and so forth, I am convinced that there is some truth in every religion, but no religion comes close to the Bible either in the amount of truth conveyed or in the purity of the teaching. The mixture of truth and falsehood is obvious, whereas the Bible is pure. As David said in Psalm 12:6, "…the words of the Lord are flawless, like silver refined in a furnace of clay, purified seven times." If you're planning a very long lifetime, you may go ahead and systematically study all the scriptures of the world. But you'll save many years if you begin with the Bible.

Authority: The Bible repeatedly identifies itself as the Word of God, and does not apologize for the fact. In other religions we find men hesitating to speak with the same authority, and saying that their words are their own views or opinions. We would certainly expect God's message to be concise and to the point. It would also be expected to identify itself as God's Word (otherwise how are we supposed to know that it's from God?)

Why do I trust the Bible? I trust it because of its remarkable preservation and transmission through the centuries. I also trust the Bible because it stands head and shoulders above all writings ever penned by man. But I trust it even more for one more vital reason: Hans, it works!

I would like to introduce you to people who have taken its message seriously and let you see the impact that it has had on their lives. Their attitudes are different, their marriages are different, their relationships are different.

Hans, I appreciate your questions, but why not begin seriously reading the Bible today, with the attitude "I'll change anything I need to" in order to find not just the Word of God, but God himself.

Hans: Jacoby, I must admit you have caused me to rethink some things. What time did you say that Bible study group meets at your house?

CONCLUSION

Clearly God has watched over his Word throughout history. As both the prophet Isaiah and the apostle Peter said, "...the word of the Lord stands forever" (Isaiah 40:8, 1 Peter 1:25).

His Word today is the same message that was preached thousands of years ago, and it is just as relevant now as then. We can have full confidence in God, and we can absolutely take him at his word!

CHAPTER SEVEN

Name One!

The "Contradictions" of the Bible

N AME ONE!" THAT'S WHAT I SAY WHENEVER SOMEONE COMES out with the familiar "Everyone knows the Bible is full of contradictions." Usually the person, caught completely off guard, cannot think of even one of the "many" contradictions he believes exist in the Bible. Other times the question may be genuine, and usually a satisfying answer can be found. Certainly I'm not implying that every part of the Bible is easy to understand, but in most cases, the "contradiction" turns out to be a misunderstanding that clears up after a second reading, or a little further study.

We saw earlier (Chapter 5) that an inconsistent revelation would lead us to doubt both God and his Word. This is why it is so important that the Bible is consistent. Now exactly what do we mean by a consistent revelation? We mean a revelation without external inconsistencies where known facts of science, logic, history, archaeology, et cetera are contradicted) or internal inconsistencies (where one part of the message contradicts another part). However, some people see inconsistencies where there are none, calling "contradictions" things that are not contradictions at all. Let's have a look at some kinds of false contradictions.

FALSE CONTRADICTIONS

I. Differences in translation among versions

No modern translation of the Hebrew and Greek text is perfect, though some versions are more accurate than others. For example, the word translated disciples (Acts 11:26) in the more accurate translations (like the NIV, RSV, KJV), is incorrectly rendered "believers" in the paraphrased Living Bible. There is, of course, no contradiction in the original text.

II. Lack of scientific precision

The Bible was never intended to be a science textbook. It often speaks of "sunrise" and "sunset," although through astronomy we know that technically it is the earth that moves, not the sun. Yet we ourselves continue to speak of "sunrise"— that does not mean that we are ignorant or "wrong."

Can you imagine Genesis 1 "In the beginning God created..." if it were rewritten scientifically: At the alpha point of space-time the Supreme Being synthesized deoxyribonucleic acid through the polymerization of polypeptides! Ancient readers would have been baffled—as most of us modern readers are! Lack of scientific precision is characteristic of the Bible's poetry—which is exactly where we take the greatest liberties in modern language! Consider Psalm 18:8-10:

> Smoke rose from his nostrils;
> consuming fire came from his mouth,
> burning coals blazed out of it.
> He parted the heavens and came down;
> dark clouds were under his feet.
> He mounted the cherubim and flew;
> he soared on the wings of the wind.

"Deoxyribonucleic what...Could you repeat that Lord?"

Physically, the heavens cannot be parted, the wind has no wings, and smoke and fire would destroy anyone's nostrils! So what? This colorful language is not a true instance of contradiction; it is poetry.

III. Approximations

We understand that the Bible often uses round numbers and other approximations—especially where large quantities are involved. (For example, Matthew 14:21, the feeding of the 5,000.) Similarly, biblical writers did not feel a burden to report the exact words when they recorded a conversation. Speeches, for example, are condensed. In fact, everything Jesus said that is recorded in the Bible can be read through aloud in just a couple of hours! Surely he spoke more that two hours in his three-year ministry, but how fortunate it is that the Bible didn't record everything: the gospels alone would be tens of thousands of pages long! Abbreviations and approximations must not be seen as contradictions.

IV. Differences with other ancient sources

For years critics laughed at the Bible because of its frequent references to the Hittites. (Remember Uriah the Hittite, the husband of Bathsheba, with whom King David committed adultery?) Because at the time there was no available archaeological evidence that the Hittites ever existed, the only record we had was God's word. Then an embarrassing thing happened for the critics: in 1906 masses of archaeological evidence for the existence of the powerful Hittite nation turned up. In the same way, the stories of Genesis were seen as legends by many historians—until valuable archaeological insights were gained in excavations at the beginning of this century, and again in the 1970s. This sort of story could be repeated many times!

Thousands of discoveries have been made confirming the record of the Bible—and yet there are still thousands of sites waiting to be explored! Since the Bible has not been proved wrong up to this point, if there's a dispute, it would seem wisest not to draw any hasty conclusions concerning contradictions.

V. Minor chronological differences

Ancient writers did not have the same concern for strict time sequence that we have. (Not that a man's death would be recorded as happening before his birth, of course!) For example, the temptations of Jesus are recorded in Matthew 4 in the order 1–2–3. Luke, however, lists them in the order 1–3–2. This is hardly a contradiction, for the details of the two temptations accounts are identical. On the whole, Bible writers were at least as careful about chronology as any other ancient writers. (See Luke 2:1–2, 3:1–2!).

72

VI. Spelling variations in different ancient manuscripts

Psalm 100:3 reads, "It is he who made us, and we are his" although earlier versions read "It is he who made us and not we ourselves." The solution: in the older translation the Hebrew word lo (his) was mistaken for the word lo (not), because of a common spelling variant. Even in English, standardized spelling is a fairly recent thing (having happened only in the last couple of centuries). For example, across the Atlantic we find hundreds of differences: honour instead of honor, tyre instead of tire, etc. No, we must not fault the various Biblical writers for grammatical, syntactical, phonological, morphological or orthological variations! These are very long words (!), but not contradictions.

VII. Minor variations from one manuscript to another

Jesus found the demon–possessed man (Mark 5:1) in the region of the Gerasenes—or was it Gaderenes? Or the Gergesenes? Scholars are not sure which reading is the original one. (But does it really matter?) No surviving manuscript is an exact copy of the original N.T. and O.T. writings, although many ancient manuscripts are near exact copies. The alternative readings listed in the footnotes of your Bible are not "contradictions" they are simply instances where translators were unsure of the correct reading. Inspiration applies to the original text, not to copies. Anyway, most differences are so minor that it would be tiresome to list them.

None of the above are true contradictions, and if we understand this we will not run into difficulty very often.

SOLUTIONS TO APPARENT CONTRADICTIONS

Following are a number of apparent contradictions. As we study each one, there will be a valuable lesson to keep in mind when you think you may have found a contradiction in the Bible.

Two Sides of a Coin

Romans 3:28 and James 2:24: In Romans, Paul says that we are made right with God "by faith apart from observing the law," while James says "You see that a person is justified by what he does and not by faith alone." Who is right, Paul or James?

The "contradiction" is so disturbing that Martin Luther, the 16th-century Protestant Reformer, decided to insert the word "alone" after faith in his personal translation of Romans 3:28. (At one point he even stated that James should be thrown out of the Bible!) But the solution is not hard to understand: true faith always proves itself in deeds or, as James says, "faith without deeds is dead" (2:26). Faith without deeds is not true faith! Neither Paul nor James is confused; what both of them wrote is inspired by God, and through their letters God tells us the truth about a right relationship with him.

In this supposed contradiction we see that the two views are really two sides of the same coin, and fit together nicely. Often a seeming contradiction resolves itself when we just take the time to be reasonable and think about it.

Missing Information

Matthew 27:45 and John 19:14: In Matthew's account by the "sixth hour" Jesus had been on the cross for some time, whereas in the gospel of John he is still before Pilate on the Stone Pavement. Did Matthew get confused, or is John the confused one? And how could their stories differ so much if they were both in Jerusalem when their Master was executed? This does not seem to be the kind of "minor" chronological difference we have discussed above.

Neither are confused! They are following different time keeping systems. Matthew, whose gospel is the most Jewish of the four gospels, is following the Jewish system of time keeping. The sixth hour is actually midday, and Jesus died at the ninth hour or 3 p.m. John, on the other hand, who is writing for a non-Jewish audience, is following the Roman method, which is like our own. In John the sixth hour was 6 a.m. After Pontius Pilate decided to have Jesus executed, the soldiers abused him for a while (Matthew 27:27)—there was still plenty of time before the crucifixion.

This particular contradiction would have been quite difficult to resolve without the missing information, which most Bibles would not supply. Again, if you have found a problem, it is probably best not to call it a "contradiction" until you have tried hard to reach a solution.

Beware of your Assumptions

Deuteronomy 34: Here we read of the death of Moses— which is remarkable, since Moses is supposed to have written Deuteronomy! This one really seems overwhelming! After all, there are only so many things a dead man can do. How did he do it?

He didn't, any more than Jesus took notes on his own crucifixion. We must be aware (or beware) of our presuppositions. It is widely believed that Moses is the author of all of Deuteronomy. If he is not, the contradiction vanishes. My own view is that while Moses was primarily responsible for Deuteronomy, edited after his death, he clearly did not write his own obituary.

Often people assume the Bible says something it never says. Contrary to popular belief, the Bible never states when the earth was created. The date "4004 B.C." was a very uninspired guess by an otherwise intelligent Archbishop a few centuries ago, but many have actually taught this as the date of creation! Let's consider some other assumptions. The Bible never says there were three wise men bearing gifts for the infant Jesus. All it mentions is that there were three different kinds of gifts (Matthew 2:11). A final example: Do you envision angels as having wings? Where does the Bible say that? It doesn't—probably we think of angels as having wings because of the Renaissance paintings.

A Little Imagination

Matthew 27:5 and Acts 1:18: About the death of Judas, in Matthew's account he hangs himself, while Luke (who wrote Acts) said that he split his intestines in a field. Who's right? (By this time you are cautious about choosing sides!)

Do we really think that Luke, the careful historian (see Luke 1:1-3) would contradict Matthew, one of Jesus' original apostles? It appears that someone (other than Judas) threw Judas' body into the field, so that it "burst open and all his intestines spilled out" (Acts 1:18). Perhaps Judas had been dead for some time, perhaps not. Or perhaps Judas fell when he was cut down from the tree from which he hanged himself—perhaps not. At any rate, the precise solution is irrelevant; there is no necessary contradiction, and it doesn't take a lot of imagination to think of a solution.

Look before You Leap!

Matthew 8:5 and Luke 7:3: In Matthew's account the centurion appears to go personally to ask Jesus to heal his servant, whereas in Luke we read that he sent some elders of the Jews to put the question to Jesus. Which is right?

Yes, they're both right. The centurion authorized the elders to go on his behalf; it was not necessary that he be there himself. In the same way, someone might say "You brought my car to the station last week, didn't you?" Would I be a deceiver if I said "That's right," even though I actually had my wife bring in the car? Isn't this an acceptable way of putting things? Of course it is.

It is possible to be overly strict in our interpretations, and we must be careful that we have the full picture before jumping to conclusions. Often a parallel passage in another part of the Bible helps to resolve the apparent contradiction. The old adage seems appropriate: "Look before you leap!"

CONCLUSION

The Bible is never at odds with science, history or logic. Science and the Bible are good friends; they work hand in glove to help us understand our world and ourselves. Nor is any discovery of historians or archaeologists going to cause the walls of Christian faith to come tumbling down! (People have tried to bring the walls down for 2,000 years, but they stand as solid as ever.) And logic: the more we think about the truth, the more likely we are to end up seeing things God's way— because the Christian faith is both true and reasonable.

The Bible has some confusing passages, but no problem disproves any of the fundamental teachings of the Bible. We should never let the parts we can't understand keep us from obeying the parts we can understand!

CHAPTER EIGHT

Don't All Roads Lead to God?

The Bible and Other Religions

D
ON'T ALL ROADS LEAD TO GOD?" "DOES IT REALLY MATTER WHICH religion you follow, as long as you believe in a higher being?" "Aren't all religions basically the same, anyway?" These are questions that many people are asking today. It's hard to see the real difference between one religion and another, and it's even harder to understand how a "loving God" would hold a difference in religion against anyone. After all, isn't it the same God we are all worshipping?

Now saying that all religions are the same is like saying all Chinese people look the same. There's one thing we know for certain about the person who says this (apart from the fact that he isn't Chinese): he's never taken a very close look at Chinese people. So it is with the world religions. Although there are occasional similarities, there are also major differences.

In this chapter we will show that all religions do not lead to God, that the world's religions are deeply divided and different from the teaching of Christ, and that in fact it matters very much which religion you follow. At first this may sound "narrow" or "exclusive," but we should weigh the evidence before deciding.

Similarities between religions are only superficial. There are several things that most religions have in common: (1) **faith,** (2) **a higher power,** (3) **obedience to that power,** (4) **attending meetings,** and (5) **a code of behavior.** But these features could just as easily apply to the realm of politics: (1) belief in the party line, (2) political power, (3) legislation and civil obedience, (4) attendance at rallies and congresses, and (5) commitment to the basic values of the party. They could also apply to: participation in a sports team, the Boy Scouts, the Rotary Club, Higher Education, and many other good institutions. I wouldn't have bothered stating the obvious, except that so many people comment that there are parallels between religions, and then stand back and wait for you to applaud their deep insight. As we shall soon see, the differences are what is significant.

Let's now turn our attention to 10 of the most significant differences between the Christian faith and other world religions:

I. **Who God Is**
II. **History and Myth**
III. **How God Speaks to Us**
IV. **Commitment**
V. **Scripture**
VI. **Evangelism of Outsiders**
VII. **Personal Morality**
VIII. **The "Golden Rule"**
IX. **Salvation**
X. **The Ultimate Goal**

I. Who God Is

Christianity teaches that there is only one God, a personal heavenly Father beyond time and space, infinitely powerful and yet intimately concerned about our lives. He loves us and sent Jesus to die for our sins. In a sense, God himself died for our sins!

No other religion understands God like this! In every other religion, man must reach up and out, and hope to attain

79

God. But in Christ God has reached down to us. He's taken the initiative.

And there are many other differences. Eastern religions like **Hinduism** and **Buddhism** identify God with the universe, so anything can be worshipped, and even we are God! Eastern religions usually accept many gods; **Hinduism** in India has more than 10,000 gods! Many of these are very human gods, sexually starved, or fat and selfish, or bloodthirsty. In Indian and Chinese religion (**Taoism** and **Buddhism**) idols are worshipped, which is seriously forbidden in the Bible. Through sacrifices the gods are pleased; we control the god, in other words.

The concept of God in **Confucianism** is very vague, and certainly not very important—what counts is worshipping your ancestors. The Buddha actually refused to comment on the existence of God, and **Buddhism** originally was an atheistic religion! The concept of God is more accurate in **Islam:** there is only one God (Allah), and he is majestic, but he's also distant from man, responsible for both good and evil, and not the personal God the Bible speaks of. In fact, since he has predestined each person to go either to paradise or to hell, fate is accepted as part of life. **Judaism** theoretically should come closest to an accurate concept of God, but Jesus Christ is rejected (even though he is spoken of in the Old Testament, which is the Bible of Judaism), and so the love of God is greatly misunderstood.

With such extreme differences, how can anyone say that we all believe in the same God? Members of many religions would be quite offended if you told them that they believed in the same God you believed in! The fact that many people use the word "God" does not mean that they all believe in the same God, any more than the fact that many people know someone named "John" means that they all know the same person!

This first major difference deserves a lot of attention, for knowing God is what Christianity if all about. (Turn back to chapters 1-3 for more information.)

II. History and Myth

In many faiths, mythical characters and legends are part of the folklore and scripture of the religion. For example, Tibetan **Buddhism** has stories of holy men flying through the air, sitting still in cold caves for months at a time without eating, and even launching hailstorms with their fingertips. The **ancient Greek religion** believed that the world was carried on the back of a super-strong giant named Atlas, while **Indian mythology** teaches that the earth is supported by four elephants on the back of a great serpent. Few Indians really believe this is true, but still the myth has a religious meaning to **Hindus.**

When we come to Christianity, everything is different. Whether miracles actually happened is very important. Whether a baby was born to a virgin in a particular country during a certain century is all-important. (The idea is important, but the idea without the fact behind it is useless.) Whether a man was resurrected from the dead is a central focus of the faith: the apostle Paul explained that if Jesus wasn't historically raised from the dead, the Christian faith is absolutely useless (1 Corinthians 15:14).

The apostle Peter insisted that the apostles, who first taught the message of Christ after his death and resurrection, knew the difference between truth and myth (2 Peter 1:16):

> We have not followed cunningly devised fables...(KJV)
> We have not depended on made-up legends...(TEV)
> We have not been telling you fairy tales...(LB)
> We did not follow cleverly invented stories...(NIV)

81

Christianity is an historical religion: either certain crucial events happened, or they didn't. Furthermore, the writers of the Bible knew the difference between history and myth, and insisted that the distinction is vital. In contrast, other religions seldom insist on this distinction. Christians know that it is so important because if God, in Christ Jesus, didn't really visit our planet and pay the penalty for our sins, there is no hope for any of us.

III. How God Speaks to Us

Here again is an area where the world's religions are deeply divided. **Christianity, Judaism,** and **Islam** urge that God speaks to man in holy scripture, while **Hinduism, Buddhism, Taoism,** and **Shinto** play down scripture and instead emphasize spiritual experience, and looking into your own heart to discover truth or God. In other words, the Eastern religions follow a more subjective standard, the Western ones a more objective standard. (Refer to our discussion in Chapter 5.)

Furthermore, in other religions, the teachings of the founder are what was originally emphasized. (Mohammed, Buddha and Confucius did not claim to be God, but pointed to the truth as they understood it.) This is not the case with Christianity: Jesus made himself the focus, not just his teachings. ("I am the way and the truth and the life. No one comes to the Father except through me," Jesus said in John 14:6.)

IV. Commitment

Most religions lay down a law or set of rules and expect their followers to obey them. Usually there is a lower expectation of commitment for the average member than there is for the holy person who devotes his full time to the religion (priest, rabbi, yogi, minister, monk, guru, et cetera.) While Christianity needs men and women to dedicate themselves to full-time service, these people are no more committed to God than those in the regular employment or courses of studies. The teaching of the New Testament is that every member of the church should do the work of the church, not just the leaders. (Every member prays, spreads the Word, learns the Bible, attends the meetings, et cetera.) This high level of commitment is very different from the commitment expected in most other religious groups.

In many religions (and sometimes even in Christianity) people try to get by with the minimum commitment, and so the result is legalism (trying to be right through law-keeping). Religion becomes just a list of do's and don't's, and if we can only be good enough then God will have to accept us. In the Koran, the holy book of Islam, Mohammed taught that we can earn Allah's mercy, earn salvation, and eventually earn paradise (40:9, 39:61, 7:43). Not that **Islam** is the only religion that teaches this; nearly every religion is a legalistic, do-it-yourself approach to God—apart from Christianity, which teaches that we are saved only through the mercy of God. However, a true appreciation of this mercy should not cause us to be lazy, but to have an even stronger commitment.

V. Scripture

With rare exceptions, in most religions the scriptures (writings) are not read—this is usually left to the "experts." This may be because in many religions the scriptures are extremely difficult to understand. The result of this is that there are not many members of other world religions who are familiar with their own scriptures. Also we should comment that the Eastern religions (Buddhism, Shinto, Hinduism, et cetera) place the least emphasis on studying scripture—which is for priests to do. Western religions (Judaism, Islam, diluted Christianity, et cetera) focus more on a holy book, but rarely stick to one book only. Judaism adds massive commentaries

(Mishnah and Talmud), Islam adds tradition more important than the Koran itself (the Hadith), while most of Christendom adds creeds, councils, statements of faith, or other authoritative writings.

The Major World Religions

Religion	Origin	Founder	Date	Scriptures
Hinduism	India	—	1500 B.C.	Vedas, Upanishads Bhagavad-Gita
Judaism	Middle East	Moses	1446 B.C.	Old Testament Mishnah, Talmud
Zoroastrianism	Persia	Zoroaster	588 B.C.	Avesta
Buddhism	India	Buddha	536-483 B.C.	Tripitaka,et cetera
Confucianism	China	Confucius	551-479 B.C.	Wu Ching Ssu Shu (with Analects of Confucius)
Taoism	China	Lao Tse	600-500 B.C.	Tao Te Ching
Jainism	India	Mahavira	540-468 B.C.	Angas, Upangas
Christianity	Middle East	Jesus	6 B. C.-27 A.D.	Bible
Shinto	Japan	—	?	Kojiki, Nihongi, Yengishiki
Islam	Arabia	Mohammed	570-632 A.D.	Koran Hadith
Sikhism	India	Nanak	1469-1538 A.D.	Granth

Christianity as we read about it in the Bible is unique in that nothing extra is added—under penalty of judgment! (Deuteronomy 4:2, Proverbs 30:6, 1 Corinthians 4:6, Revelation 22:18-19.) It's the Bible plus nothing—and the personal responsibility of every follower is to digest and spread it.

For other major ways in which the Christian Scriptures (found in the Bible) are different from other world scriptures, see the end of Chapter 6.

VI. Evangelism of Outsiders

Most religions are not concerned with winning others to their position. **Judaism** is extremely inward focused, and rarely has converts. **Hinduism,** with its loose concept of truth, does not teach its followers to go and make disciples. **Buddhism** soon became a missionary religion, but few Buddhists today consider evangelism a priority. The same is true of nearly every religion, fundamentalist **Islam** being the notable exception. (Muslims are an exception because they firmly believe that they are right, and that no one else has the hope of going to heaven.) Christianity, in the same way, is radically different from most religions, especially in Jesus' teaching that all his followers are to actively make followers (or disciples) of every nation (Matthew 28:19-20).

Interestingly, the people who proclaim "All roads lead to God" most loudly are those who are afraid to spread the Word!

VII. Personal Morality

Here is yet another area in which we find tremendous differences among world religions. Most religions officially discourage drunkenness, bad language, gambling, premarital sex, and other actions, but unofficially tolerate them, because they are unable to give their members the determination—or the power—to live morally. With Christians it is a very different situation.

Because every Christian in the local community (the church) is striving to live the moral life Jesus lived, there is much more incentive—and mutual help—to change.

The code of ethics Jesus preached in his famous Sermon on the Mount (Matthew 5-7) is second to none, with its emphasis on loving enemies and pure-heartedness, and not even thinking evil. When questioned about which parts of the Old Testament were the most important, Jesus pointed to the commands to love God with all our heart and to love our neighbors as ourselves (Matthew 22:37-40). Perhaps this is why Christianity, more than any other religion, has done so much to help the poor.

All other religions have a lower standard of personal morality. **Islam** has wife beating, polygamy, concubines, and holy wars (Jihad), all authorized in the Koran (Surahs 4, 24, 8). **Hinduism** has its lusting gods and goddesses and rigid caste system which seriously discriminates against the poor. Hinduism, teaching that all suffering is the result of evil actions in previous lives, and **Buddhism,** with its insistence that suffering is unreal, have allowed millions to suffer alone. **Shinto** has no real concept of morality at all, but speaks rather of duty. But Christianity demonstrates the highest standard of personal morality, for the goal is to be like Jesus (1 John 2:6).

Don't be confused: there is a distinction between true Christians (disciples who are actually putting Christ's teaching into practice, are committed, and are spreading the faith) and people who only call themselves "Christians," but are not fully committed.

VIII. The "Golden Rule"

Jesus' saying, "So in everything, do to others what you would have them do to you" (Matthew 7:12) has been called the "Golden Rule." Other religions (**Confucianism** and **Judaism**) have the "Negative Golden Rule," which is "Don't do to others what you wouldn't want them to do to you." Which is easier?

Christ taught that we should actively love our neighbors. In other words, rather than wait for convenient opportunities to do good to others, we should make opportunities to help others. Most people proclaim "I try to mind my own business and not hurt anyone else," as though this were exemplary behavior. It is not exemplary at all; if that is all we do, it is quite unloving and selfish. For those whose eyes are open, there are always loads of opportunities to help meet others' physical, emotional, and (especially) spiritual needs.

IX. Salvation

As we have already seen, salvation cannot be earned or deserved. It is God's gift to man, There is no way to "work" our way to God. But what is "salvation?" Salvation from what?

In **Islam** salvation is freedom from hellfire. In **Hinduism** it is escape from the endless cycle of death and rebirth ("reincarnation"). In **Buddhism** it is the blissful realization that our "self" is only an illusion, that we have no independent existence. In **Judaism** there is little concept of salvation, other than freedom from hardship. In the Christian faith, however, salvation is freedom from sin and death. Other religions speak of sin to some extent, but only Christianity offers real hope: Jesus Christ dying on the cross in our place. It should be clear that although most religions have some concept of "salvation," there is no agreement at all over what "salvation" is.

X. The Ultimate Goal

Do all religions lead to the same place? By now it should be plain that they do not. In **Christianity** the goal (heaven) is knowing God; in **Islam**, being rewarded by God in a paradise of wine, women and song; in **Hinduism**, absorption into God and loss of personal identity; in **Buddhism**, loss of all desire and realizing that there is no God, and no you; in other religions, discovering that you were God all along! How can we say that all religions have the same goal? As someone has said, if all religions lead to God, how come most of them, having been given a thousand years at least, haven't yet arrived?

CONCLUSION

Our findings about the Bible and other religions:

- The differences far outweigh the similarities.
- The Bible stands alone among the scriptures of the world.
- All roads do not lead to God.
- Jesus is indeed the only way to God, as he taught.

As an ancient Jew once wrote about the Word of God, "Your word is a lamp to my feet and a light for my path" (Psalm 119:105).

Yes, there is a way to God, but if we are going to find the way we'll need help from God's Word. That sort of light comes only from the Bible. In summary, other religious systems are a set of swimming instructions for a drowning person; Christianity alone offers the life preserver!

Before we can make our informed decision, there is one last bit of evidence that must be considered: the resurrection of Jesus Christ from the dead. So on to Chapter 9!

CHAPTER NINE

Many Convincing Proofs

Miracles and the Resurrection

T HIS CHAPTER FOCUSES ON THE RESURRECTION OF CHRIST FROM the dead. Jesus predicted that he would rise from the dead—and he did! As the historian Luke says in Acts 1:3:

After his suffering, he showed himself to [the apostles] and gave many convincing proofs that he was alive. He appeared to them over a period of forty days...

In the second part of the chapter we will look at the overwhelming evidence that Jesus Christ did in fact come back from the dead—and hence must be the Son of God, just as he said he was. The proof of the resurrection was extremely convincing and helpful to me as I considered becoming a Christian, and I believe that you too will find it helpful. But first, some clarification on the subject of miracles.

MIRACLES

That's Impossible!

One reason why people laugh at the miracles of the Bible is that they have already concluded that miracles are impossible. Their line of reasoning goes something like this:

1) Miracles would break the laws of nature.
2) The laws of nature cannot be broken.
3) Therefore miracles are impossible!

Now about (1), I suppose that is true, if we define a miracle as an act (of God) which breaks the laws of nature—or speeds up the laws of nature, or in some other way goes against scientific laws. Obviously a card trick is not a miracle, nor an eclipse of the sun, nor the many coincidences that all of us have experienced.   Miracles are, by definition, unusual and extraordinary —if they happened all the time they would not be miracles.

I also agree that (3) follows logically from (1) and (2). But what has not been shown is that (2) is true. (And how could it ever be proven? It is only an assumption.) If there were no God then I believe that "miracle" would be a meaningless term, one which would apply to anything we didn't understand. But, as we have seen, there is conclusive evidence that there is a God: in the person of Jesus Christ—and also in miracles. Since there is a God, it is reasonable that there are miracles too.

Watch out for Counterfeits!

Once while playing a video game (Pac-Man) I reached and tried to put another 50-pence piece into the machine. The coin jammed so badly that the owner of the machine called the police, who demanded to know where I had got this counterfeit coin from. (Criminal Offense!) But when I explained that I was a Christian minister and started to invite the big police sergeant to church, they released me, warning me to watch out for counterfeits.

There are many counterfeits in this world—mere forgeries. From coins and checks to Renoirs and Rembrandts, from passports and wills to diamonds and gold, counterfeiting is here to stay.

So it should not surprise us that most present-day "miracles" are counterfeit. These "miracles" are common in every religion of the world including some that call themselves "Christian." Most of these claims are exaggerations and lack any proof at all. Jesus warned us against those who do false miracles (Mark 13:22-23). Let us be wise.

Wisdom, however, does not mean rejecting all miracles as false. The miracles of the Bible are entirely different from "miracles" of other religions, or the tricks we see today. For example:

- They were undeniable and accepted even by enemies of the faith (John 11:47).
- They were performed publicly by men of known integrity; there was never any appeal for money (Acts 8:20).
- They were not done to stun or thrill, but to bring important spiritual truths from God to man (Mark 16:20).

God can do miracles, and I am not saying that he doesn't answer prayer today, but let's watch out for counterfeits!

Is Your God Too Small?

In case you are still thinking, "I believe in God, but I am not sure that God could do miracles," I believe that you have a problem: Your God is too small! Many people stumble over the idea of miracles not because they are being illogical, or even stubborn; they just don't have a proper concept of God. You see, an infinitely powerful God outside of space and time would find it no more difficult to create a world, inspire a book, or raise a man from the dead than you would to breathe air or tie your shoe. Is your God too small?

Are You Sure You Want to See a Miracle?

It's easy to think that if only we could see a miracle, then we would really believe in God and Jesus and become committed Christians. But this way of thinking is highly unrealistic.

Imagine Jesus Christ paid you a visit tonight! At 3 a.m. he comes and stands by your bedside; you are startled by the brilliant light in the room, and behold the Son of God! You ask him all your questions, he answers, you feel very spiritual. He commands you to obey him, you promise to try hard, he goes back to heaven and you go back to sleep.

This experience would be very vivid for a few days, but can't you hear the voice of doubt at the second or third week? (Are you sure it wasn't a dream? Couldn't it have been a hoax? Is there any scientific proof for his visit?) Unless you had made a very firm decision in your heart to follow God, it would be very easy to talk yourself out of obeying him. That is exactly what many people did in the lifetime of Jesus.

He performed many, many miracles during his three-year ministry, but what was the number of his faithful followers after his death and resurrection? Only 120 (Acts 1:15)! Are we really that much more spiritual than hundreds of thousands of men and women who heard Jesus speak and saw him perform miracles, and yet even talked themselves out of following him? Are you sure you want to see a miracle? Would you really be prepared to make a total commitment to Jesus Christ? Let's not be unrealistic.

Principles to Keep in Mind

Here are some important facts about miracles:

- Many modern "miracles" are not miracles at all.
- If there is a God, true miracles are possible.

- Witnessing miracles does not guarantee future obedience.
- Excitement about miracles easily causes wrong motivations.
- God wants us to base our faith on reason, not sensation.
- No miracle can possibly convince us if we're unable to be convinced!

The unique miracles of the Bible are recorded for a reason: so that we can learn about them and have faith in Christ:

> Jesus did many other miraculous signs in the presence of the disciples, which are not recorded in this book. But these are written so that you may believe that Jesus is the Christ, the Son of God... (John 20:30-31).

THE RESURRECTION: The Greatest Miracle of All

It is Crucial!

Listen to the firm words of the apostle Paul on the resurrection:

> For what I received I passed on to you as of first importance: that Christ...was raised on the third day according to the Scriptures, and that he appeared to Peter...to the Twelve...to more than five hundred of the brothers at the same time...to James...to all the apostles...and to me also... (1 Corinthians 15:3-8).

The resurrection is crucial to the entire Christian message. It is "of first importance," as Paul says. Then he insists that Christ appeared to many people, giving "many convincing proofs" (Acts 1:3). Listen to how Paul responds to some who water down the reality (and the significance) of the resurrection:

> And if Christ has not been raised, our preaching is useless and so is your faith. More than that, we are then found to be false witnesses about God...And if Christ has not been raised, your faith is futile; you are still in your sins...Then those who have fallen asleep [died] in Christ are lost. If only for this life we have hope in Christ, we are to be pitied more than all men...If the dead are not raised, "Let us eat and drink, for tomorrow we die!" (1 Corinthians 15:14-19, 32).

Now either the resurrection happened, or it didn't; and either Jesus appeared after his death to a great number of people, or he didn't. Remember, Christianity is a historical religion, based on real historical events. To attack the resurrection is to attack the very heart of the Christian message! Furthermore, if Christ was not raised:

- Preaching is useless.
- Christians are liars.
- Christian faith is useless.
- Our sins are still unforgiven.
- The dead have no hope of salvation.
- Christians are the most pathetic men in the world.
- We might as well seek pleasure, since life is so short.

Let's consider these points, since Paul states them so emphatically. Many religious people would try to talk you out of your belief in the resurrection, if they could. They insist that the Christian message and faith are still valuable, whether or not Christ was raised. They would never call Christians "liars," since they diplomatically hesitate to tell anyone that they think he might be misled. As for forgiveness, they are quite sure that anyone can be saved, whether or not he has responded to Christ.

And they insist, very spiritually, that even if there is no heaven, we shouldn't live selfishly, but still remain Christians. But their definition of "Christian" is very weak, and they do not at all mean what you mean by that word.

94

What a contrast to this way of thinking the biblical message of the resurrection is! It's as though we are being openly invited to disprove the resurrection. If the resurrection fails, the whole faith falls!

This chapter does not try to explain all the miracles in the Bible, for if we can accept the astounding miracle of the resurrection, we can certainly accept all the other, easier, miracles. The Christian faith is open to investigation—indeed, it *begs* you to investigate!

The Proof of the Resurrection

Now that we understand the claims of Jesus stand or fall on the resurrection, we should be eager to weigh the evidence for it. If you're not familiar with the story of the crucifixion and resurrection of Jesus, you will find them in Matthew 27:26-28:15, Mark 15:15-16:14, Luke 22:63-65, 23:26-24:12 and John 19:1-20:28. Select one of these accounts and become familiar with it.

Following is a diagram of the logical possibilities. It will be helpful to keep referring back to this diagram as you read about the evidence.

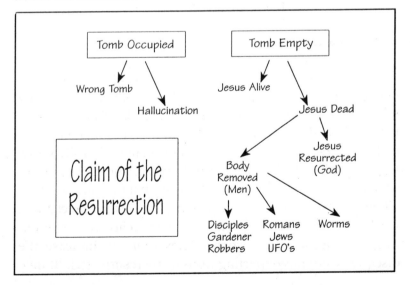

We begin with the claim of the resurrection. This is one thing everyone is agreed on: that the early Christians claimed it happened. Whether or not Jesus was resurrected, the question of the tomb remains: either the tomb was occupied, or it was empty. Let's assume first that it was occupied all along. If it was occupied, there are two possibilities: (a) the first people who proclaimed the resurrection went to the wrong tomb, or (b) possibly all the appearances were merely hallucinations.

Wrong Tomb Theory

The theory was invented by a Harvard professor, who thought that perhaps in the dawn the women (Matthew 28:1) accidentally went to the wrong tomb. But is it really likely that they went to the wrong tomb on Easter Sunday? Or that none of the other disciples could remember the location of the new tomb, like Joseph of Arimathea, who owned the tomb (Matthew 27:60) and personally buried Jesus (John 19:42)? Sooner or later someone would have discovered the right tomb—which is the downfall of this explanation.

Hallucination Theory

This is a variation of the previous theory, since a hallucination (mental illusion) would be totally unconvincing if the physical body of Jesus were still available for inspection. It is possible that one or two of the more emotional disciples hallucinated—but would all of them imagine that they saw Jesus? (Hallucinations are most common among people of similar personality types.) Moreover, hallucinations occur when someone is hoping or expecting to see the object about which he hallucinates. (Like a thirsty man in the desert imagining he sees an ocean.) However, in this case the disciples were not expecting Jesus to be resurrected. If they had been, they would have been lined up at the tomb on Sunday morning, since Jesus had predicted many times that he would rise from the dead on the third day (Matthew 16:21, 20:19 et cetera). But they were not at the tomb, for they did not expect Jesus to rise; the crucifixion for them was not the prelude to the resurrection, but the death of a dear friend. They expected no comeback (John 20:19).

Another great weakness of the Hallucination Theory is the claim of Paul in 1 Corinthians 15:6, where he claimed that most of some 500 eyewitnesses were still alive. (A foolish claim to make if they were still around and could be independently questioned!) Yet the greatest weakness remains that which we mentioned at first: the unsolved problem of the empty tomb. Where was the body? If everyone went to the tomb (presumably even the Romans guarded the wrong tomb), why didn't the opponents of the faith simply produce the corpse of Jesus?

The Wrong Tomb Theory and the Hallucination Theory are both poor attempts to avoid the problem of the empty tomb—and the missing body. The actual tomb of Jesus was definitely empty.

The Swoon Theory

This theory proposed that Jesus never really died on the cross, but was mistaken for dead. After lying in the cool tomb for a few days, he revived and appeared to his disciples, causing them to mistakenly believe that he had risen from the dead. There are several grave weaknesses in this attempt to explain away the resurrection:

- It assumes that Jesus deceived his disciples (by allowing them to mistakenly believe that he was raised). But would this be in character with Jesus? Was he really a deceiver?

- It assumes that Jesus could have survived some 36 hours in the dark, cool tomb, having been wrapped up in linen and 75 pounds of preservative ointments (John 19:39), without food or water!
- It ignores the trauma (physical and emotional shock) that Jesus had been through before being entombed: a sleepless night, clubbing, torture, flogging, the crown of thorns, punching, weakness to the point that he stumbled under the weight of his own cross, crucifixion (nails being driven into his wrists and feet), and the final spear thrust of a Roman soldier into his heart (John 19:34). In fact, Jesus died long before he was laid in the tomb!
- It assumes that the Roman soldiers (experts in execution) were confused about whether Jesus was alive or dead. The executioners observed that the two thieves crucified along with Jesus were still alive, and so they broke their legs to speed up their deaths, but they decided not to do this in the case of Jesus, since they were convinced that he was already dead (John19:32).
- It assumes that Jesus, weakened by the crucifixion and then immobilized in linen wrapping, still had the strength to stand on his feet, roll the large stone away, overpower the Roman guards, walk miles and miles on pierced feet and then manage to convince his doubting disciples that he had conquered death and risen from the dead! (This is getting ridiculous!)

The swoon theory refutes itself. No, logic and the Scriptures alike tell us that Jesus was truly dead on the cross. The body was missing from the tomb that resurrection morning; this much is certain.

Who Moved the Body?

If this question can be answered, the resurrection can safely be dismissed as Christian fabrication. But if there is no satisfactory answer, only one alternative remains: Jesus rose from the dead.

Deceitful Disciples?

The earliest explanation of the resurrection by unbelievers was the Jewish story that the disciples were sleeping (Matthew 27:62-66, 28:11-15). Yet why should we suppose that they removed the corpse and then proclaimed that Jesus had risen from the dead? This would mean that the disciples stole and lied, both violating the clear teaching of their Master. It would mean also that they died for a lie. From time to time a person of great conviction will die for something he thinks is true (like Buddhist monks who set themselves on fire in protest of the Vietnam War, or Shiite Muslims who believe that dying in the service of Allah guarantees a place in heaven—but who would knowingly die for a lie? Remember how Jesus' disciples suffered for the faith:

- Paul and James (John's brother) were beheaded.
- Andrew and several others were crucified in the usual way.
- Peter was crucified upside down.
- Nearly all the disciples were flogged, beaten and persecuted.

No, men may sincerely die for the wrong thing, but none will die for something they do not believe in! Furthermore, that the disciples would change from timid and ineffective men (John 20:19) to powerful preachers of Christ is psychologically extremely unlikely. (What can account for the dramatic change except the resurrection itself?) Besides, how would eleven cowardly men (Judas had committed suicide) take on a well armed-Roman guard assigned to guard the tomb? And would the guard really sleep on the watch? (See Acts 12:19,

16:27.) We can safely conclude that the disciples could not have stolen the body.

Early Bird Gardener?

Again we must determine the motivation for removing the body. Jesus' body was laid in a private tomb and there was a gardener to take care of the garden, but why would he move it at such an early hour (dawn) Sunday morning? And how could he have overcome the detachment of Roman guards? (Did his shovel and trowel prevail against the sword and shield?) Breaking the seal of Pilate (Matthew 27:66) would have been a serious crime, an offense against the Roman state. And even if he did remove the body, why didn't he reveal where it was once the resurrection was preached? Surely a friend of the Christians would have shown the body in order to spare them the persecution they were suffering, whereas a foe would have revealed its whereabouts to stop the rapidly growing Christian faith. The gardener too can be declared innocent!

Thoughtless Thieves?

Completely ignoring the difficulty posed by the Roman guards, why would grave robbers take the body? Grave robbers look for valuables, not corpses or linen. There was nothing of value buried with Jesus, and even if there was, who would steal a corpse weighing some two hundred twenty pounds (counting the ointments and linens)? The suggestion that grave robbers stole the body of Jesus is ludicrous!

Rebellious Romans?

Now why would the Romans take the body? (Absurd!) There is, again, no motive. The Romans were concerned with keeping the Jews (and the Christians) peaceful and quiet. So why would they do something that would launch the Christian faith into its initial growth spurt? They wouldn't. The Romans certainly did not remove the body.

Jealous Jews?

The Jews are the last ones on earth who would have taken the body, since they tried everything to stop the preaching of the resurrection (Acts 5:28, 40). If they had possessed the body of Jesus, all they would have needed to do would be to put the corpse on a cart, pull it through the streets of Jerusalem, and shout "Yes, he is risen indeed!" Since the body would have been the single most valuable evidence they could have used to stop the spread of the faith, clearly it was not in their possession. (The possibilities are becoming fewer and fewer!)

Sorceress Saucers?

The wildest theories about the resurrection come from the pens of Science Fiction writers. Since there is no evidence whatsoever that UFOs lifted the body from its resting place, and it is obvious that we are now proposing solutions beyond rational discussion, we will leave this suggestion where it belongs.

Starving Worms?

It is getting very hard to come up with any convincing solution for the disappearance of the dead body of Jesus. Did hungry worms eat it up (over a short weekend)? Doesn't it make a lot more sense to abandon these wild attempts to explain away the resurrection?

Jesus Rose from the Dead!

The sober truth makes much more sense than the many attempts to explain away the truth. Let's retrace the steps we've gone through:

1) The tomb had to either be occupied or empty: we saw that it was certainly empty.

2) Jesus had to be either dead or alive when his body was placed in the tomb: we saw that he was certainly dead.

3) The body was either removed by others, or resurrected by God himself: we saw that as others could not have taken the body, the resurrection is the only sensible explanation.

In light of all the evidence, it takes more faith not to believe in the resurrection than to accept it as true. Truly, Jesus rose from the dead! This is the only explanation which makes sense of all the facts, including Jesus' repeated prediction that he would rise on the third day. It is also the best explanation for the incredible transformation in the lives of the early disciples, as well as in the lives of all true disciples today.

If the resurrection happened, (1) Jesus is exactly who he said he was, (2) there is no good reason why less incredible miracles in the Bible could not have occurred, and (3) we must all respond personally to the resurrection:

> In the past God overlooked such ignorance, but now he commands all people everywhere to repent. For he has set a day when he will judge the world with justice by the man he has appointed [Jesus]. He has given proof of this to all men by raising him from the dead (Acts 17:30-31).

CHAPTER TEN

True and Reasonable!

Making An Informed Decision

IF YOU ARE LIKE ME, BEFORE READING YOUR FIRST EVIDENCES book you probably had no idea that there was so much convincing evidence for the Christian faith! (The fact is, this book could easily have been ten times longer, since we only scratched the surface of the overwhelming amount of evidence in favor of the Christian position!)

Two facts have been demonstrated in this book:

- God is real.
- The Bible is his Word to us.

In other words, Christianity is both true and reasonable . Unfortunately, though, not everyone is ready to accept this. Remember Festus:

> ...Festus interrupted Paul's defense. "You are out of your mind, Paul!" he shouted. "Your great learning is driving you insane." "I am not insane, most excellent Festus," Paul replied. "What I am saying is true and reasonable" (Acts 26:24-25).

Festus, who was not a believer in Jesus, was personally challenged by Paul's testimony. Notice, however, that he did not consider Paul to be brainless—just a bit mad. And from the perspective of the unbelieving Festus, he was a bit mad. But Paul, in full control of himself, insists that the message of Christ is both true and reasonable.

Now it is our turn; we must respond. There are two changes which must take place in our lives:

- **We must have faith.** (Your faith should already be much stronger after considering the evidence.)
- **We must make an informed decision.** (It's not good enough just to believe. As we saw in the last chapter, God expects us all to repent, or give our lives to him.)

We have seen that becoming a Christian is not a leap into the dark, but actually a leap into the light, since the evidence is so heavily on the Christian side. Now that we know the truth, are we going to be reasonable? That's our decision.

Becoming a Christian disciple is not something to be rushed into—on the other hand, it is urgent that we make our informed decision as soon as possible. My prayer is that every reader who is not a Christian will make that decision in the very near future.

If you're considering becoming a Christian, you can find out what God requires by reading the book of Acts. (It is here that we find many accounts of men and women becoming Christians.) Finally, I would encourage you to find a committed Christian who can teach you more about the Bible, whom you can trust to challenge you to give your best to God.

For Additional Study

Suggested Reading

EXISTENCE AND NATURE OF GOD

Clayton, John N., **Does God Exist?**
I believe that the reader will find all the written and cassette tape material in this series helpful. Available from 17411 Battles Road, South Bend, IN 46614.

Miethe, Terry L. and Habermas, Gary,
Why Believe? God Exists!
College Press (Joplin, Missouri)

Packer, J. I., **Knowing God**
Hodder & Stoughton (London)

Philips, J. B., **Your God is too Small**
Macmillan (New York)

Schaeffer, Francis, **He Is There and He Is Not Silent**
Tyndale (London)

GENERAL

Hoover, Arlie, **Dear Agnos**
Baker (Grand Rapids, Michigan)

Lewis, C. S., **Mere Christianity**
Fontana; Collins (Glasgow)

Lewis, C. S., **The Screwtape Letters**
Collins (Glasgow)

Little, Paul E., **Know Why You Believe**
Anzea (London)

McDowell, Josh, **Evidence that Demands a Verdict**
Campus Crusade (San Bernadino, California)

McDowell, Josh, **He Walked Among Us**
Campus Crusade (San Bernadino, California)

McDowell, Josh, **More than a Carpenter**
Tyndale (London)

McGuiggan, Jim, **If God Came**
Montex (Lubbock, Texas)

Paley, W., **Evidences of Christianity**
Parker (London)

Schaeffer, Francis, **How Should We Then Live?**
Crossway (Westchester, Illinois)

Smith, W. M., **Basic Christianity**
InterVarsity Press (London)

Story, Dan, **Defending Your Faith**
Thomas Nelson (Nashville, Tennessee)

Wharton, E. C., **Christianity: A Clear Case of History**
Howard Book House (West Monroe, Louisiana)

MIRACLES AND RESURRECTION

Anderson, J. N. D., **Evidence for the Resurrection**
InterVarsity Press (London)

Green, Michael, **Man Alive!**
InterVarsity Press (London)

Lewis, C. S., **Miracles**
Macmillan (New York)

McDowell, Josh, **The Resurrection Factor**
Here's Life Publishing, Inc. (San Bernadino, CA)

Morrison, Frank, **Who Moved the Stone?**
Zondervan (Grand Rapids),
Faber & Faber (London)

OBJECTIONS AND PROBLEMS

Bruce, F. F., **Jesus & Christian Origins Outside the New Testament**
Hodder & Stoughton (London)

Dowsett, Dick, **"God, That's Not Fair!"**
O. M. F. (Sevenoaks, Kent)

Lewis, C. S., **The Problem of Pain**
Macmillan (New York)

Russell, Bertrand, **Why I Am Not a Christian**
Simon and Schuster (New York)

SCIENCE AND PHILOSOPHY

Abbot, Edwin, A., **Flatland**
Blackwell (Oxford)

Clayton, John N., **The Source**
(17411 Battles Road, South Bend, IN 46614)

Denton, Michael, **Evolution: A Theory in Crisis**
Adler & Adler (Bethesda, Maryland)

Hayward, Alan, **Creation and Evolution**
Triangle (London)

Johnson, Phillip, **Darwin on Trial**
InterVarsity Press (Downers Grove, Illinois)

Ramm, Bernard, **The Christian View of
Science and Scripture**
Paternoster Press (London)

Ross, Hugh, **The Creator and the Cosmos**
NavPress (Colorado Springs)

Schaeffer, Francis, **Escape From Reason**
InterVarsity Press (London)

Schaeffer, Francis, **Genesis in Space and Time**
Hodder & Stoughton (London)

Sire, James, **The Universe Next Door:
A World View Catalog**
InterVarsity (Downers Grove, Illinois)

Vestal, Daniel, **The Doctrine of Creation**
Convention Press (Nashville).

SCRIPTURE

Archer, Gleason, **Encyclopedia of Bible Difficulties**
Zondervan (Grand Rapids, Michigan)

Bruce, F. F., **The New Testament Documents: Are They Reliable?**
InterVarsity Press (London)

Bruce, F. F., **The Books and the Parchments**
Pickering & Inglis (London)

Lightfoot, Neil R., **How We Got the Bible**
Sweet (Austin, Texas)

Packer, J. I., **God Has Spoken**
Hodder & Stoughton (London)